# THE WAY OF THE CROSS

(Formerly Published as *Beyond Humiliation*)

## A CONTRIBUTION TO THE DOCTRINE OF CHRISTIAN SANCTITY

by

## J. Gregory Mantle

Kingsley Press

Shoals, Indiana

*The Way of the Cross by J. Gregory Mantle*

PUBLISHED BY KINGSLEY PRESS
PO Box 973
Shoals, IN 47581
USA
Tel. (800) 971-7985
Web: www.kingsleypress.com
Email: sales@kingsleypress.com


ISBN: 978-0-9719983-2-2


Second Kingsley Press Edition: 2007


Distributed in the United Kingdom by:
Harvey Christian Publishers, UK
11 Chapel Lane
Kingsley Holt
Stoke-on-Trent, ST10 2BG
England
(01538) 756391
Email: sales@harveypublishers.co.uk


Cover design by Ed Ulyate


Printed in the United States of America

*I lovingly*
*inscribe this volume*
*to the memory*
*of my*
*father and mother*

# Contents

*Let him that readeth these things be content with what he feeleth thereof suitable to his own present estate. And as the Life grows in him and he in the Life, and he comes to meet with the things and exercises spoken of, the words and experiences concerning them will, of themselves, open up to him, and be useful and serviceable to him so far as the Lord pleaseth; he keeping to the leadings, savor, and principle of Life in himself wherein alone his knowledge, sight, growth, and experiences are safe.*

—Isaac Pennington

# Publisher's Foreword

Since its first appearance in 1896, this little volume has gone through numerous editions and at least two titles. For many years it was known as *The Way of the Cross,* but more recently many have come to know it under the title *Beyond Humiliation.* In preparing the present edition for the press, we have used the First Edition of 1896 as a basis, because we felt that most of those interested in obtaining and reading this volume will want to possess all twenty-three chapters of the original version in their unabridged form. To the best of our knowledge, *every* edition since the first has omitted at least two chapters. *Beyond Humiliation* omits not only the customary two chapters, but also various paragraphs here and there throughout the book.

By stating the above, we are not criticizing any former publisher for not presenting an unabridged work, but rather making it clear that this edition is an exact copy of the original.

I wish to express my profound gratitude to Jack Morrison of Rare Christian Books for his kindness in loaning me his copy of this book for us to reprint from, and for his encouragement along the way.

The only changes that have been made are that American spelling has been used throughout, all Roman numerals for Scripture references have been changed to ordinary numbers, and in a very few instances punctuation has been updated.

In his Preface to the Second Edition of this book, Gregory Mantle wrote: "Many testimonies have reached me from far and near of definite blessing received through pondering these pages. To God alone be all the glory." May the Lord add to that number many in this generation who can testify to receiving the same blessing from perusing these pages.

Edward Cook
Kingsley Press
March, 2004

Is thy heart athirst to know
That the King of heaven and earth
Deigns to dwell with man below,
Yea, hath stoop'd to mortal birth?
Search the Word with ceaseless care,
Thou shalt find this treasure there.

For if Christ be born within,
Soon that likeness shall appear
Which the heart had lost through sin.
God's own image fair and clear,
And the soul serene and bright
Mirrors back His heavenly light.

Jesus, let me seek for nought
But that Thou shouldst dwell in me;
Let this only fill my thought,
How I may grow liker Thee,
Through this earthly care and strife,
Through the calm eternal life.
                              —LAURENTIUS LAURENTI

CHAPTER 1

# The All-Methodical God

NO originality is claimed for this title. Readers of Professor Adam Smith's *Isaiah* will remember that on several occasions in the first volume of his Commentary he calls attention to the word ambiguously translated *"judgment,"* and reminds us that the word means *method, order, system, law;* so that when we read in chapter 30:18, that "the Lord is a God of judgment," Isaiah means that God has His own way and time for doing things, and that, "having laid down His lines according to righteousness and established His laws in wisdom, He remains in His dealings with men consistent with these."

"It is a great truth," says he, "that the All-mighty and All-merciful is the All-methodical too; and no religion is complete in its creed, or healthy in its influence, which does not insist equally on all these."

A full recognition of the orderliness of God in His working would save us from much of the disappointment which we now experience, and greatly increase the healthiness and consequent power of true religion.

Let us spend a few moments over this suggestive fragment of history. Alarmed by Isaiah's predictions of the siege of Jerusalem, the Jewish politicians were startled into doing something. Instead, however, of returning in penitence to God, and relying upon Him in the time of their threatened trouble, they sought to accomplish an expensive and profitless alliance with Egypt. What scorn Isaiah pours upon this suicidal intrigue!

Then he pictures the caravan which Judah sent with tribute to Egypt. In a few graphic strokes he gives us to see asses and camels carrying their riches through the land of trouble and anguish, through lions and vipers and fiery-flying serpents, to a people that will only deceive and disappoint them, for "Egypt helpeth in vain, and to no purpose, therefore have I called her *Rahab Sit-Still"* (30:1-8).

It was not *alliance* they needed, as Dr. Smith says, but *reliance;* for "Thus saith the Lord God, the Holy One of Israel, In returning and rest shall ye be saved; in quietness and in confidence shall be your strength; and ye would not…. And therefore will the Lord wait, that He may be gracious unto you; and therefore will He be exalted, that He may have mercy upon you: for the Lord is a God of method: blessed are all they that wait for Him."

We sometimes congratulate ourselves on the cleverness and ingenuity of our plans, as the princes of Judah did in this instance; but Isaiah reminds them that "God also is clever, and will bring evil, and will not call back His words" (31:2). Until we have learned that no individual, church, or nation can play tricks with God, that He has His own way and time of doing things, He will *wait,* that He may be gracious; and blessed are they who turn away from Egypt, with her chariots and horsemen, and *wait for Him.*

The great sin of man has always been in this direction, a preference of his own will to the will of God; a preference of his own inclinations for God's obligations. It is the sin of the Church today, and the explanation of her enfeebled and pitiable position in the eyes of the world. When we think we have discovered a short and easy road to success, and have forsaken the Fountain of living waters to hew out to ourselves cisterns, we shall always find that our hewing has been labor lost, and that our cisterns are broken and will hold no water.

Does the Church of Jesus Christ think she can accomplish God's work in the world without a definite experience of heart purity and the Pentecostal baptism? It is admitted that the early Christians were thus made usable to the Master; but there is an impression abroad that this qualification for successful service can be dispensed with in these days. The result is failure, disheartenment, disappointment; for the Lord is a God of method. The Holy Spirit waits to show men and women how the Cross of Christ is the pathway of complete deliverance from the guilt and power of sin; and He will stand aloof from His people while they cherish those "low views" with which, as Faber says, it is as easy for the devil to contend against God as with mortal sins.

These "low views" of sin and of privilege explain the pride, the passion, the selfishness, the envy, the jealousy, the resentment, the barrenness, the worldliness, the secret sympathy with sin over which thousands of really converted people mourn, and from which they sometimes think there is no deliverance. And God is raising up, all over the land, witnesses to His power to effect a "double cure," not only to save from wrath and to pardon actual transgressions, but to deal with that moral depravity which lies further back and deeper down in our nature, and is at the fountain-head of all character and activity.

What command could be more imperative and explicit than that which the risen Christ gave to His disciples: "Tarry ye until ye are endued with power from on high"? They dare not go forth to their work without this power. To have done so would have been to court defeat and to expose themselves to ridicule. When they were thus equipped they reached the maximum of their usefulness, men and women were saved by thousands, and the kingdom of Christ advanced by leaps and bounds. Then the Church formed an alliance with the world; she laid her head in the lap of Delilah, and being shorn of her true strength, began making frantic efforts to do her work without the all-essential credentials. Those credentials are the possession of power over all the power of the enemy; and we vainly imagine that abiding work can be done in our pulpits, Sabbath schools, mission halls, or in any other direction, by activity *minus* the power of the Holy Spirit. Sooner or later we shall awake to the fact that the Lord is a God of method, and that blessed are all they that wait for Him.

Let us ponder, in conclusion, the four words which the prophet here uses to indicate in what direction their salvation lay, and upon what terms they might be sure of the Divine interposition and abiding protection.

The first is the word "*returning.*" Instead of going to Egypt for help, and impoverishing themselves by an alliance forbidden, senseless, and unprofitable, they might be assured of God's forgiveness and favor by returning in brokenness of spirit to Him. Have we any reason to expect any large outpouring of the Holy Spirit until we too return in true and deep penitence to God? *The place of confession is the place of forgiveness.* It is here God is pledged to meet us, and nothing is more striking throughout the history of this rebellious and wayward people, than God's readiness to forgive and restore them to His favor on the first indication of true repentance. "Remember from whence thou art fallen, and repent and do the first works, or else. . . ." Immutable is the promise: "Return unto Me, and I will return unto you." The God All-methodical is the God All-merciful. He waits *that He may be gracious.*

The next word is *"rest."* The meaning is, of course, such a resting in God as would prove the genuineness of their return to Him. Vain was their reliance on the multitude of chariots and the strong body of cavalry to which they would point as a valuable addition to the fighting strength of Judah; for, as Isaiah reminds them, "The Egyptians are men, and not God; and their horses flesh, and not spirit." When Jehovah stretches His hand both the helpers and the helped shall fall, and they shall all perish together (31:3).

Rest! Thousands of hearts are longing for it! And it cannot be found, as some vainly dream, by flying away on the wings of a dove from their surroundings. Rest comes through a true confession and determined forsaking of sin, and through the cleansing of the nature from its stains, for sin in every form is *dis-ease,* the opposite of rest. Material things are in a state of rest while fulfilling the laws and purposes for which they exist. The least variation of adjustment results in disquietude instead of repose. So rest comes to man through an adjustment of his will to the will of God. "Take My yoke *(i.e.,* My will) upon you. . . and ye shall find rest unto your souls." The Romans forced their enemies to put their neck under a yoke as a sign of defeat. Hence we get the word *subjugate—sub,* under; *jugum,* a yoke. Rest comes through the subjugation of the whole being to Jesus. The perfect emblem of rest is God, and in proportion as man has his center in God he becomes a partaker of His rest (Heb. 4:3).

The third word is *"quietness."* How the very word rebukes the haste, excitement, and trepidation with which they had prepared for the siege of their city! *"He that believeth shall not make haste."* What so surely indicates the feebleness of our grasp of these eternal truths as the fretted, harassed, feverish lives so many of us live! When all occasion for war has been put away, and we drink deep draughts of heavenly life, we shall know what has been called "the high pressure of the Holy Ghost," which is not contrary to that reposeful and quiet spirit which characterized the Lord Jesus Christ, and which He means us also to possess.

The fourth word is *"confidence."* The word means the assurance and courage which comes of the settling down of the soul upon one who is known to be true and trustworthy. "They that know Thy name will put their trust in Thee" (Psalm 9:10). To know God is to trust Him; to know Him perfectly is to have that perfect confidence in Him which alone inspires courage, and is the secret of all true spiritual strength. "In *confidence* shall be your *strength.*" There are two departments in the school of grace where this confidence is acquired, and in both of them the pupils must be taught: one is the word of God, and the other is the walk with God. What can explain the confidence of Judson, and many another noble missionary, working steadily on for years without any sign of visible success, but this settling down of the spirit upon God—an attitude which had, with them, become a habit of life?

As we learn to tread the way of the Cross we shall enter more fully than ever into the meaning of Paul's words: "We are the circumcision, who worship by the Spirit of God, and glory in Christ Jesus, and have no confidence in the flesh" (Phil. 3:3). And loss of confidence in ourselves will be followed by a constant glorying in Jesus as the source of all our life, the secret of all our strength.

Multitudes have yet to learn that the God All-methodical is, to those who practically recognize Him as such, the God All-mighty; and to be continually stayed upon Him is restfulness, quietness, confidence, and strength.

Oft have I wished a traveler to be:
Mine eyes did even itch the sights to see
That I had heard and read of.
At last I said: "Go travel first thyself.
Thy little world can show thee wonders great:
The greater may have more, but not more neat
And curious pieces. Search and thou shalt find
Enough to talk of. Make no pretences
Of new discoveries whilst yet thine own
And nearest little world is still unknown.
Away, then, with thy quadrants, compasses,
Globes, tables, maps, and minute glasses!
Lay by thy journals and thy diaries!
Close up thy annals and thy histories!
Study thyself and read what thou hast writ
In thine own book—thy conscience!" Is it fit
To labor after other knowledge so,
And thine own nearest, dearest self not know?
Travels abroad both dear and dangerous are,
Whilst oft the soul pays for the body's fare.
Travels at home are cheap and safe. *Salvation*
*Comes mounted on the wings of meditation.*
*He that doth live at home, and learns to know*
GOD *and himself, needeth no further go.*

—CHRISTOPHER HARVEY

# CHAPTER 2

# A Mixed Life

IN the beginning a threefold separation was accomplished before the command was given: "Be fruitful, and multiply." God separated the light from the darkness, the waters beneath from the waters above the firmament, the sea from the dry land; and to show His jealousy for physical order still further, He forbid an Israelite to plough with an ox and an ass under the same yoke (Deut. 22:10). Mixed garments were also strictly forbidden: "Thou shalt not wear a garment of divers sorts, as of woollen and linen together" (Lev. 19:19). Wool and linen come from separate kingdoms in nature, one from the animal, the other from the vegetable, and unmixedness of moral character is clearly foreshadowed. To wear, in the same robe, the wool of selfishness and the linen of spirituality is contrary to the law of order which prevails in the kingdom of grace as in the kingdom of nature. God is as jealous—nay, more jealous—of moral order than of physical order; and, as Dr. Denney says, "Is it not a great thing, a worthy thing, that we should set ourselves to purge away from our whole nature, outward and inward, whatever cannot abide the holy eye of God; and that we should regard Christian holiness, not as a subject for casual thoughts once a week, but as the task to be taken up anew, with unwearying diligence, 'carrying holiness to completion in the fear of God!'"[1] Most Christians, as he says, make a beginning, and cleanse themselves from obvious and superficial defilements of the flesh; but how few carry the work on *into the spirit*.

This thought of unmixedness is still further illustrated in the dress of the priests: "When the priests minister in the inner court, they shall be clothed with linen garments; no wool shall come upon them while they minister in the inner court, and within" (Ezek. 44:17). To enter "within the veil" and dwell there in the presence of God, there must be a laying aside of all that appertains to the dark world—the world of our

15

selfhood—and our nature must be clothed with the fine linen, clean and white, which is the righteous acts of the saints and the robing of the Bride of Christ (Rev. 19:8).

Few will deny that this mixedness in Christian life and work is a great bane, and seriously interferes with the effectiveness of both. This was Paul's trouble in the Corinthian Church. The Christians were possessed of a regenerate babe-life which Paul calls "carnality." They lived a kind of suspended life, now dominated by the flesh and now by the Spirit, and the result was an elementary experience, envying, strife, and division (1 Cor. 3). Those who are living this mixed life are spoken of as double-minded (more exactly double-souled) men (James 1:8; 3:8). There is only one cure for such a condition. It is the converging of all the desires and affections in the same center, viz., the love of God's will and glory. When this is the case true singleness of heart is experienced. "If thine eye be single, thy whole body shall be full of light."

Before we can live the unmixed life, and belong no longer to the carnal but to the spiritual Christians, we must be willing to know the extent of the mixedness in our own nature, for what the eye does not see the heart will not grieve over. Before we invite God to search us, let us pause and ask whether we are willing that He should make a thorough work of this self-discovery, however painful and humbling it may be? If not, we had better not begin; for it is better to be without the light than to possess it and be disobedient.

For obvious reasons no branch of knowledge is so neglected as knowledge of ourselves. In other sciences knowledge flatters the vanity of the unsanctified heart; it exalts men in the eyes of others, it increases their influence in the world. But true self-discovery wounds our pride, and spoils the good opinion we had formed and cherished of ourselves. We may be skilled in every other science and ignorant in this. We may be able to calculate the motions of the heavenly bodies, and know nothing of the movements of our own sinful nature. We may be able to plant our foot on a mountain summit where no human foot has ever before trod, and yet be ignorant of the dimensions of the black mountain of self in our heart. We may be able by chemical analysis to detect and decompose the material substances around us, and yet never analyze the motives by which we are influenced, and which color and stain all our conduct.

"Self-love conspires with trust in our own hearts to make dupes of us as regards our spiritual account. Proverbially, and in the verdict of all experience, love is blind; and if love be blind, self-love being the strongest, the most subtle, the most changeless, the most difficult to eradicate of all loves, is blinder still. Self-love will not see, as self-trust cannot see, anything against us." It is this ignorance that leads to quiescence. The hateful foe assumes such disguises, and appears so exactly the opposite of what he really is, that we lose sight of the fact that he is a devil still, and that, as Luther was wont to say, the white devil is more to be dreaded than the black.

What is necessary then, since self-love will cause us to live in such a fool's paradise if we follow its interested opinion, is the search-light of God. This, and this alone, will disturb our self-complacency and self-deception. "Because thou sayest, I am rich, and have gotten riches, and have need of nothing; and knowest not that thou art the wretched one and miserable and poor and blind and naked: I counsel thee to buy of me gold refined by fire, that thou mayest become rich; and white garments, that thou mayest clothe thyself, and that the shame of thy nakedness be not made manifest; and eye salve to anoint thine eyes, that thou mayest see" (Rev. 3:17, 18, RV).

The two great pillars upon which true Scriptural Christianity rests are the greatness of our fall and the greatness of our redemption. "Until," says William Law, "you are renewed in the spirit of your mind, your virtues are only *taught practices* and grafted upon a corrupt bottom. Everything that you do will be a mixture of good and bad; your humility will help you to pride; your charity to others will give nourishment to your own self-love, and as your prayers increase so will the opinion of your own sanctity. Because till the heart is *purified to the bottom,* and has felt the axe at the root of its evil (which cannot be done by outward instruction), everything that proceeds from it partakes of its impurity and corruption."[2]

Nothing is easier than self-deception; few things are so difficult as real self-disclosure. We may be claiming and even professing the experience of holiness, and yet know nothing of a total death to the carnal or natural life. The dress and conversation of the inhabitants of Canaan are imitable; but the true divine life is as inimitable as life always is.

Let us not mistake phraseology for experience, the maiming of the enemy for his death, sanctimoniousness for sanctification, unctuousness for unction, or the knowledge of the truth for the Spirit of truth, for "when truths have once been fully revealed and been made a part of orthodoxy, the history of them does not necessarily imply an operation of the Spirit of God."

There is a striking thought in the literal translation of Hebrews 4:13: "Neither is there any creature that is not manifest in His sight: but all things are naked, and lying open unto the eyes of Him with whom we have to do." The passage might be rendered: "All things are stripped and stunned," the figure being that of an athlete in the Coliseum, who has fought his best in the arena, and has at length fallen at the feet of his adversary, disarmed and broken down in helplessness. There he lies, unable to strike a blow or lift his arm. He is stripped and stunned, disarmed and disabled, and there is nothing left for him but to lie at the feet of his adversary, and throw up his arms for mercy. It means not only the stripping off of all covering and concealments, but the lying prostrate in exposure before the eye of God (Alford). That is what the Holy Spirit and the searching Word will do for us if we are willing, and until we are willing, we shall be living a mixed life, with more or less of self, and more or less of Christ.

O Lord, when Thou didst call me, didst Thou know
    My heart disheartened thro' and thro',
    Still hankering after Egypt full in view
Where cucumbers and melons grow?
                  —"Yea, I knew."

But, Lord, when Thou didst choose me, didst Thou know
    How marred I was and withered too,
    Nor rose for sweetness nor for virtue rue,
Timid and rash, hasty and slow?
                  —"Yea, I knew."

My Lord, when Thou didst love me, didst Thou know
    How weak my efforts were, how few,
    Tepid to love and impotent to do,
Envious to reap while slack to sow?
                  —"Yea, I knew."

Good Lord, Who knowest what I cannot know,
    And dare not know, my false, my true,
    My new, my old; good Lord, arise and do,
If loving Thou hast known me so.
                  —"Yea, I knew."

—CHRISTINA ROSSETTI

# CHAPTER 3

# "Examine Me, O Lord!"

THE power of the kingdom of sin rests in self-deceit, and, as we have already suggested, self will not tell tales about self. Much so-called self-examination is therefore not only of no advantage to a Christian, it is a positive hindrance to his progress in the life of holiness. Bushnell tells of a lad he knew, who had undertaken to grow a patch of watermelons. He looked to see them ripen long before they were grown. He went to them every day, examined and tested them, pressing his thumb down hard upon them to see if the rind would snap, for that was to be the sign when they were ripe. But the poor things, under so many indentations, fell to rotting and did not ripen at all. They were examined to death. God's sun and wind and rain and dew were doing a much better examination. So with regard to that undiscovered continent—the uncleansed nature. However often we may engage in the exercise of self-examination, we shall be deceived and discouraged, because we are utterly disqualified for the task. God's sunshine, God's wind and rain and dew, will do the work effectually. In other words, what God's Light reveals His Spirit will remove. "The Lord is my Light and my Salvation." Not the light without the salvation, for that would overwhelm me, and not the salvation without the light, for that would inflate me.

A well-known spiritual teacher specifies seven varieties of self-deceit. Among them he mentions the complacent self-deceit. Men whose infallibility is the fixed point of their compass. Men who find an external reason for every failure which no foresight could have calculated, and against which no prudence could have guarded. They are not only receiving inspirations every moment, but cross inspirations. But they take this very easily, almost as if it were a feature of divine guidance. They are so unchangeably changeable that it is quite easy for them to believe themselves consistent, when everybody else thinks them not to be depended on in the commonest matter.

Another form of self-deceit is censoriousness. They are men who are always so sure that they are right, that they set themselves up as a standard by which to judge others. To abstain from doing this would, in their estimation, be an act of false humility. Such persons are always on the judgment seat, as if they came into the world for the sole and express purpose of judging others.

Then there is that odious form of self-deceit which is falsely humble. "The pride that apes humility is the devil's darling sin." The saintliest of the virtues is thus counterfeited. Such people are always speaking ill of themselves, not in the least believing what they say, for it is possible for a man to speak of himself in terms the most reproachful in the spirit of supreme egotism. This kind of self-deceit stoops to conquer, and though it wears the garb of the utmost self-abasement, it affects to be stripped of self only that it may gain the praise of men. "Come and see my humility" is the language of such a man, and though he deceive himself and others by his dress, the first flash of divine light shows him to be wrapt round with the stolen livery of an angel of light while full of the leprosy of sin.

Professor Rendel Harris has called attention to the fact, that this affectation of humility is one of the ways in which souls are constantly kept out of blessing. "The true humility says, when the Lord has made a feast and bidden His guests, 'I shall go and take the *lowest* place;' but the affected humility says, 'Oh! it's too good for me; I shall sit down outside;' and so, practically, it becomes numbered amongst those of whom it is said, 'They shall not taste of My supper.'"[1]

These are only a few of the manifold varieties of self-deceit, and we may well despair of drawing it from its hiding-places, and chasing it through all the latent mazes of our being with any skill or power of our own. He who longs to have us all for Himself, and whose jealousy for His own is such that He will not leave a divided heart in peace, who has so made us that the least affection outside of Himself complicates our lives, and causes us to feel ill at ease, will undertake this work for us, not doing it in any superficial or imperfect fashion, but putting us in the crucible till all the dross and alloy of our nature have been brought to light. He waits to have us put that word to the proof: "I will turn My hand upon thee, and purely purge away thy dross, and take away all thy alloy" (Isa. 1:25).

This disclosure must be made some day, for the corruptible life of self cannot inherit incorruption, and towards this old Adam nature, in all its repulsive or seemingly innocent features, our God is a consuming fire. Yet the work is such that, as we have several times said, we must count the cost before we pray, "Lord, show me myself," for "who may abide the day of His coming? and who shall stand when He appeareth? for He is like a refiner's fire, and like fuller's soap: and He shall sit as a refiner and purifier of silver, and He shall purify the sons of Levi, and purge them as gold and silver; and they shall offer unto the Lord offerings in righteousness." We must give Him time for His work, for He makes no slight or passing business of it; He will *sit* as a refiner. We must not start at the *suffering* it entails, for that is what the purging as gold and silver means. As fire burns out the slag and sifts it from the sound metal, as a chemical lye (fuller's soap) eats out impurities, so He will gather out the true heavenly life, and burn up the chaff of self with unquenchable fire.

My God! my God! and can it be
    That I should sin so lightly now,
And think no more of evil thoughts
    Than of the wind that waves the bough?

I sin, and heaven and earth go round
    As if no dreadful deed were done;
As if Thy blood had never flowed
    To hinder sin or to atone.

Shall it be always thus, O Lord?
    Wilt Thou not work this hour in me
The grace Thy passion merited,
    Hatred of self and love of Thee?

O, by the pains of Thy pure love,
    Grant me the gift of holy fear;
And by Thy woes and bloody sweat,
    O wash my guilty conscience clear.

Ever when tempted make me see,
    Beneath the olives' moon-pierced shade,
My God, alone, outstretched, and bruised,
And bleeding, on the earth He made.

And make me feel it was my sin,
    As though no other sins there were,
That was to Him who bears the world
    A load that He could scarcely bear.

CHAPTER 4

# The Light of the Cross

"THE school of the Cross," said John Bunyan when he was dying, "is the school of light." It is the mirror in which the selfishness, hideousness, and penalty of human sin is reflected. There is no searchlight like that which flashes from the hill of Calvary for discovering to us the plague of our own hearts.

Simeon's words which predict the sorrows that were to pierce Mary's heart, predict also the laying open of the hidden dispositions of many other hearts (Luke 2:34, 35). Our deepest self is revealed by our attitude to the Cross of Jesus. If we stand in its light, we shall find it a touchstone where we are tried and proved to the very depths of our being. It will be "quick and powerful, and sharper than any two-edged sword, piercing even to the dividing asunder of soul and spirit, and of the joints and marrow, and a discerner of the thoughts and intents of the heart. Neither is there any creature that will not be manifest in its sight."

The Cross is not only possessed of sin-killing, but of sin-discovering power. Before it can be "death to every vice," it must be light to reveal its loathsomeness. When Mark Antony wanted to inflame the Roman populace against the assassins of Julius Caesar, he lifted up the dead Emperor's garment and said:

> You all do know this mantle: I remember
> The first time ever Caesar put it on;
> 'Twas on a summer's evening in his tent;
> Look! in this place, ran Cassius' dagger through;
> See, what a rent the envious Casca made:
> Through this, the well-beloved Brutus stabb'd,
> And, as he pluck'd his cursed steel away,
> Mark how the blood of Caesar follow'd it.

25

To see what your sin really means bring it into the light of the Cross, and say as you gaze upon that marred visage and those pierced hands and feet: "It was *my* pride, *my* lust, *my* unbelief, *my* selfishness, that pointed the nails and fixed the thorns." There are those who can testify that the perceived relation of the death of Christ to their sin has instantly so discovered to them its true character, and has so broken its power that the Cross has proved in an utterly unexpected sense their pathway to freedom.

A Bechuana Christian exclaimed in the enthusiasm of his newly-found faith: "The Cross of Christ condemns me to become a saint!" His words contain an all-important truth, for they at once reveal the real purpose of the Saviour's death and the true object of the Christian's life. That object is not the forgiveness of sins, not a title to heaven, not deliverance from the wrath to come, but a saintly walk. Yes, the Cross condemns me to become a saint.

It is out of the light of the Cross that men who profess to be Christians, and who have perchance renounced glaring sins, drop into a slothful, selfish, worldly life. They contrast their present with their past; or they compare their life with the lives so many are living around them, and they are content. The danger of this condition is intensified, because in gross sin there is some prospect of getting the conscience disturbed, but in this unhealthy state they persuade themselves that this is all that is required of them, and all that Jesus can do for them, and they cry: "Peace, peace, when there is no peace!"

St. Paul meets the horrible suggestion, "Shall we continue in sin that grace may abound?" with the words: "God forbid. How shall we, that are dead to sin, live any longer therein? Know ye not, that so many of us as were baptized into Jesus Christ were baptized into His death?" (Rom. 6:1-3). That surely means that Christ's death implies union as well as substitution. His death and resurrection-life condemn me to be a saint, and it is unspeakably mean of me to claim to be one with Him in the freedom from sin's punishment, which His Cross secures, and not one with Him in His attitude towards sin and in His attitude toward God. Dean Vaughan speaks strongly when he says: "All sinning now is a re-crucifixion—it is a disregard, it is a despite, it is more—it is a re-binding and re-nailing and re-torturing and re-agonizing and re-killing of Him whose one death was the sufficient sin-bearing, and therefore the intended sin-eradication and sin-extermination for ever."[1]

Yet this crime of perpetual crucifixion is continually enacted in the thought-life of the world, and with this awful aggravation: the men of the first century knew not what they did, they sinned in the dark, but the men of the nineteenth century sin against the light. "The criterion of character," says one, "is moral identification," and if our life belies our lips, if we make an orthodox profession but live a heterodox life; if we trifle with what we ignorantly call little sins and allow them to have dominion over us; if we are cowardly and silent, and given to desertion as the Christ of God stands at the bar of public opinion; if we not only refuse to confess Him ourselves, but hinder others from confessing Him, we morally identify ourselves with those who cried: "Away with Him; not this man, but Barabbas!"

"It was not the hammer and the nails which crucified Him; nor the Roman soldiers who wielded the weapons of His passion; nor the arm and the hand which smote the sharp iron into the wood—these were but the blind material instruments of His agony. His true crucifiers were our sins—and we, ourselves—the sinners, for whom He died. This was the real power of darkness which set in motion all the array of death. Wilful sins renew, in virtue and by implication, the wounds that were suffered on Mount Calvary. And this reveals in us the true depth and measure of our guilt."

Oh, what pains, and what a death it is to nature, to turn me, myself, my lust, my ease, my credit, over into "my Lord, my Saviour, my King, and my God, my Lord's will, my Lord's grace!" But alas! that idol, that whorish creature *myself* is the master-idol we all bow to. What hurried Eve headlong upon the forbidden fruit, but that wretched thing *herself?* What drew that brother-murderer to kill Abel? That untamed *himself.* What drove the old world on to corrupt their ways? Who, but *themselves,* and their own pleasure? What was the cause of Solomon's falling into idolatry and multiplying of strange wives? What but *himself,* whom he would rather please than God? What was the hook that took David and snared him first in adultery, but his *self-lust?* and then in murder, but his *self-credit* and *self-honor.* What led Peter on to deny his Lord? Was it not a piece of *himself,* and *self-love* to a whole skin? What made Judas sell his master for thirty pieces of silver, but the idolizing of avaricious *self?* What made Demas to go off the way of the Gospel to embrace the present world? Even *self-love* and a love of gain for *himself.*

Every man blameth the devil for his sins; but the great devil, the house-devil of every man, the house-devil that eateth and lieth in every man's bosom, is that idol that killeth all, *himself.* Oh! blessed are they who can deny themselves, and put Christ in the room of themselves! O sweet word: "I live no more, but Christ liveth in me!"

—SAMUEL RUTHERFORD

CHAPTER 5

# The Idol Self

WE are told in the history of India, that Mahmoud—who conquered a great portion of India hundreds of years ago—destroyed all the idols in every town to which he came. In time he laid
siege to the great city of Guzurat. Forcing for himself an entrance into
the costliest shrine of the Brahmins, there rose before him the figure
of a gigantic idol, fifteen feet high. He instantly ordered it to be destroyed. The Brahmins of the temple prostrated themselves at his feet,
and said: "Great Mahmoud, spare our god, for the fortunes of this city
depend upon him."

> "Ransom vast of gold they offer, pearls of price and jewels rare,
> Purchase of their idol's safety, this their dearest will he spare.

> "And there wanted not who counselled, that he should his hand
>     withhold,
> Should that single image suffer, and accept the proffered gold."

But Mahmoud, after a moment's pause, said he would rather be
known as the breaker than the seller of idols, and struck the image with
his battle-axe. His soldiers followed, and in an instant the idol was broken to pieces. It proved to be hollow, and had been used as a receptacle
for thousands of precious gems, which, as the image was shattered, fell
at the conqueror's feet.

> "From its shattered side revealing pearls and diamonds, showers of gold;
> More than all that proffered ransom, more than all a hundred fold."

Such an idol is self, who pleads and promises that "if we wilt but
let it to stand, it has pleasures, gifts, and treasures to enrich us at command." This hateful idol will spend years in intriguing to escape from

29

the hand of God. Not in listening to its pleadings, however, but in de-livering the idol over to utter destruction, shall we find our true wealth and pleasure, for jewels of priceless worth await those who have learned the secret of losing their life for Christ's sake that they may find it.

Utter abandonment to God is, then, the only way of blessing. The alabaster vase must be broken that the ointment may flow out to fill the house. The grapes must be crushed that there may be wine to drink. Whole, self-centered, unbruised, unbroken men are but of little use, they "abide alone," living lives of isolated selfish indifference to every-one but themselves. They murmur at God's providences, because self is disturbed in its enjoyment; they are easily offended and difficult to reconcile, because their self-esteem has been wounded; they thirst for and eagerly drink in the flattery and praise of men because it indulges self-love; they are proud and egotistical, because they love to worship at the shrine of self; they are reluctant to give wealth or time to God's work in the world, because they want the latter for their own ease and the former for their own enjoyment. The nemesis of such a life is that, shrinking from death *to* self they die *in* self, for there must be a total loss of self, either in God and for Him, or without Him.

The way of the Cross means, then, the overthrow of egoism, for before the divine life can rise in man, self must die. It is the very ground and root of sin. The assertion of the *I* is the perpetual tendency of the flesh. "I live" is the watchword of carnalism, and there is no sin which is not an assertion of self as the principle of life. This idol is able to assume so many disguises, some of which are so subtle, delicate, and refined, that its presence in the heart can only be discovered by that search-light of the Holy Ghost of which we have spoken.

It was at this idolatry of self, under the garb of religion, that Christ hurled the most terrible denunciations that ever fell from His lips. It was known in His day as Pharisaism, and wherever the life finds its center in the I, we are in danger of becoming as offensively egotistical as they.

This idol may actually assume the character of a defender of holi-ness teaching, and we may be ready to fight over terminology, and say the bitterest things of those who dare to think differently to our-selves. That was why the Pharisees hated Christ, and hounded Him to the death of the Cross. Our Christian work, our prayers in public and private, our reading of the Scriptures, our almsgiving, may all become poisoned with Pharisaism, and utterly devoid of the graciousness, meekness, and self-forgetfulness of Jesus Christ, and poisoned they inevitably will be, if the idol self is not given over to that glorious idol-breaker, Jesus Christ, for destruction.

"Who can tell," says one, "what harm this I does to devotion—how it lessens it, and narrows it; how it renders piety ridiculous and contemptible, in the eyes of the world, which is always ready to criticize, spitefully and pitilessly, the servants of God? Who can tell of how many miseries and weaknesses and falls it is the cause? How it makes devout people fretful, uneasy, officious, uncertain, eccentric, jealous, critical, spiteful, ill-tempered, insupportable to themselves and to others? Who can tell how often it frustrates and stops the operations of Divine grace; how it favors the cunning and snares of the devil; how it makes us weak in temptations, cowardly in times of trial, reserved and ungenerous in our sacrifices; how many noble designs it brings to nought; how many good actions it infects with its dangerous poison; how many faults it disguises and makes appear as virtues?"

This idolatry of the human I is, then, to be fought against, and pursued through all the intricacies of our being, with bitter, unrelenting hate. Self is the very citadel of Satan in the heart; it is the great stronghold of the enemy; it is the most subtle, the most stubborn, the most tenacious foe with which the Holy Spirit has to contend in our nature. "Self," says William Law, "is not only the seat and habitation, but the very life of sin; the works of the devil are all wrought *in self; it is his peculiar workhouse;* and therefore Christ is not come as a Saviour from sin, as a destroyer of the works of the devil in any of us, but so far as *self* is beaten down and overcome in us. Christ's life is not, cannot be, within us, but so far as the spirit of the world, self-love, self-esteem, and self-seeking are renounced and driven out of us."

This is absolutely necessary to re-establish the order of God. Our disordered self must be seen in God's light, and His work can only be accomplished by a dispossession of ourselves. It is this continual death to self which constitutes the life of faith. It is so sweet a death, that we may sing of "the pain and bliss of dying," because the grace which gives perfect peace, takes the place of nature which brings constant trouble. It is a state, moreover, in which God communicates Himself with familiarity. When we forsake it we grieve the Holy Spirit; and God makes us feel that we are deprived of Him as soon as we turn from Him to the creature, and that by so doing we have rendered ourselves unworthy of His intercourse.

> What has stripped the *seeming* beauty
> From these idols of the earth?
> Not the sense of right, or duty,
> But the sight of nobler worth.
>
> Not the crushing of those idols,
> With its bitter pain and smart,
> But the beaming of *His* beauty,
> The unveiling of *His* heart.
>
> 'Tis the *look* that melted Peter,
> 'Tis the *face* that Stephen saw,
> 'Tis the *heart* that wept with Mary,
> Can alone from idols draw.
>
> Draw, and win, and fill completely,
> Till the cup o'erflow the brim;
> What have we to do with idols
> Who have companied with Him?

Made for Thyself, O God!
Made for Thy love, Thy service, Thy delight;
Made to show forth Thy wisdom, grace, and might;
Made for Thy praise, whom veiled archangels laud;
Oh strange and glorious thought, that we may be
A joy to Thee!

Yet the heart turns away
From this grand destiny of bliss, and deems
'Twas made for its poor self, for passing dreams,
Chasing illusions melting day by day;
*Till for ourselves* we read on the world's best,
"This is not rest!"

Nor can the vain toil cease,
Till in the shadowy maze of life we meet
One who can guide our aching, wayward feet
To find Himself, our Way, our Life, our Peace.
In Him the long unrest is soothed and stilled;
Our hearts are filled.
—F. R. HAVERGAL

# CHAPTER 6

# Self and Sin

ONE of the most striking features of the recent teaching of holiness is the prominence which has been given to the absolute necessity of claiming deliverance from the self-life ere the true life of God can appear in men. We should be thankful for this, for if the Adversary can succeed in persuading us that a paste jewel is a diamond of the first water, he will be greatly rejoiced while we shall be woefully disappointed. The fruit of the Spirit will not be seen until in the unity of our Lord's sacrifice we have gone down with Him into the dark grave, and heard Him say: "I am the Resurrection and the Life; he that believeth on Me, though he were dead, yet shall he live."

Nothing has done so much to discredit the teaching of holiness as the unlovely, censorious, self-assertive spirit that has, alas! been so often displayed by those who have professed to know the experience. God's cloth-of-gold has sometimes become cloth-of-dust. The explanation lies very largely in the failure, on the one hand, to appropriate complete deliverance from every taint of the plague of self, and on the other to "put on the Lord Jesus" as the unfading robing of the new life.

More than two hundred and fifty years ago, Francis de Sales found it necessary to utter a warning word on this subject. "It is a delusion," he says, "to seek a sort of ready-made perfection which can be assumed like a garment; it is a delusion, too, to aim at a holiness which costs no trouble, although such holiness would no doubt be exceedingly agreeable to nature. We think that if we could discover the secret of sanctity we should become saints quickly and easily."

Perhaps it is because we have attempted to make saints too quickly and easily that we have had in so many cases an experience that has been a disappointment to the possessor, to the onlookers, and above all to God.

The eye of the world is quick to perceive any indication of selfishness in those who profess to be wholly given up to God, and while it is sometimes complained that the standard they set up for God's saints is too high, it is quite possible that ours may be far too low. If we are truly delivered from the plague of selfishness, we shall not kick against injustice; we shall not stand upon our rights; we shall not manifest any self-important bearing, or cherish any resentful spirit. We shall not be elated when praised, or disheartened when blamed. We shall not thrust ourselves in the best seat in the train or tramcar. We shall always be ready to wash the feet of the saints; we shall not seek to do great things, but gladly do the least and lowliest service. We shall not be offended if others are preferred before us; we shall not get feverish about the present or worried about the future; we shall not seek to get the best of a bargain. We shall never, as the Welsh preacher said, "put our hand into our Master's till," or so speak of ourselves or our achievements as to attract attention to ourselves rather than to Jesus Christ. In all these things He has left us an example that we should follow His steps, and to be truly holy is to be truly Christ-like.

To be saved from the leprosy of sin is, therefore, to be saved from the leprosy of self, and if we are not saved from the latter, we are certainly not from the former. "Self," says Law, "is the root, the branches, the tree of all the evil of our fallen state." "Every act of sin," says Westcott, "being in its essence self-regarding and self-centered, must be a violation of love. Thus lawlessness is, under another aspect, selfishness; or as it is characterized by St. John, 'hatred in opposition to love.'" "Sin and lawlessness are convertible terms. Sin is not an arbitrary conception. It is the assertion of the selfish will against a paramount authority."[1] "Sin is the voluntary separation of the soul from God: this implies the setting up of the law of self actively, and passively the surrender to internal confusion."[2] "Sin is the moral attribute of selfishness, or the choice of self-indulgence as the end of life."[3]

In order that we may see that this self, which we are called upon to hate and renounce, is no phantom, we will dwell on one of its principal manifestations, self-love.

The love of ourselves and desire for our own happiness, when kept within due bounds, is natural and innocent, for it is not natural for a man to hate his own flesh. It is when this principle passes its appropriate limits that it becomes selfishness. Selfishness was the sin of the first angel "who rested in himself," as Augustine says, instead of referring himself to God.

The soul, in the exercise of its affections, must have a center of love somewhere. That central object has the heart's affections, whatever its character may be. The center of man's love must be either in himself, in other creatures, or in God. He may love all, but he cannot love more than one supremely. If this love *centers* in self, the man is of course a selfish being, and cannot be a holy being, for holiness is the antithesis of selfishness. Pure love is not inordinate, that is, it is precisely such a measure of love as the object is entitled to. When God has circumcised our heart to love Him with all our heart and with all our soul, that we may live (Deut. 30:6), everything will fall into the right position; self will be cast out of the soul, we shall love God supremely, and we shall love ourselves and other beings just as God would have us.

If love, when centered on self, is allowed to increase, it becomes open rebellion and disobedience. This is what Augustine calls "the love of self carried so far as to despise God." Self-love is then the sworn foe of the love of God. No one can dispute His claim to be loved absolutely by us, in Himself and for Himself. As it is contrary to His law to allow a creature to prefer self to God as a center, and as it is contrary to His nature not to hate sin, He must hate self-love, which is the very soul of sin, and the plague spot from which all other sins proceed.

Self-love is not only the enemy of God, it is also our own. By turning us away from our only good, we are deprived of that intimate communion with God without which we can never be at rest, for God cannot admit us to His immediate presence until self-love has been completely conquered, and He has become all in all.

We must learn to make God what He has made Himself—the end of all things; and so to do this that at any time we can turn round upon ourselves and say of our life, at any moment and in any of its outgoings, "God is my end!" Everything that does not revolve round Him as its center is doomed to destruction, and will be found to be wood, hay, and stubble in the day when every man's work shall be made manifest—when the fire shall try every man's work of what sort it is.

Note in Luke 12:15-21 an illustration of a life lived in independence of God. In the self-congratulatory speech which Jesus puts into the mouth of this supreme egotist the word "my" occurs five times. It was "*my* fruits," "*my* barns," "*my* corn," "*my* goods," "*my* soul." God was in none of his thoughts. Note, also, God's estimate of this self-centered life and the Saviour's application, "*So is everyone* that layeth up treasure for *himself* and is not rich toward God."

There is a similar illustration in the Old Testament of one whose name means fool, Nabal (see 1 Sam. 25:11). It was "*my* bread," "*my* water," "*my* flesh," "*my* shearers." Nothing may be meant when we talk about "my work," "my mission," "my address," "my sermon," "my gift," but the habit is a dangerous and insidious one, and unconsciously we may be nourishing the hateful self-life, instead of refusing to make any provision for it.

"O my God, selfishness is Thy enemy. It is also mine, a mortal enemy bent on my destruction. Thou hatest selfishness, and I desire also to hate it. Thou hast commanded its destruction as Thou didst command the destruction of Agag. Grant me grace not to spare Thy enemy, but to permit Thee to wage war upon it. I love Thee, O my God, and I wish to love Thee as I ought—with all my heart and mind and soul and strength. Circumcise therefore my heart with Thy two-edged sword, that henceforth I may be Thine and Thine alone."

What is it to be inwardly crucified? It is to be dead to every desire, whatever it may be, which has not the Divine sanction; to be dead to every appetite and every affection which is not in accordance with the Divine law; to have no desire, no purpose, no aim but such as comes by Divine inspiration, or is attended with the Divine approbation. To be inwardly crucified is to cease to love Mammon in order that we may love God, to have no eye for the world's possessions, no ear for the world's applause, no tongue for the world's envious or useless conversation, no terror for the world's opposition. To be inwardly crucified is to be, among the things of this world, "a pilgrim and a stranger"; separate from what is evil, sympathizing with what is good, but never with idolatrous attachment; seeing God in all things and all things in God. To be inwardly crucified is, in the language of Tauler, "to cease entirely from the life of self, to abandon equally what we see and what we possess, our power, our knowledge, and our affections; that so the soul in regard to any action originating in itself is without life, without action, and without power, and receives its life, its action, and its power from God alone."

—PROFESSOR UPHAM

# CHAPTER 7

# The Inward Cross

THE French have a most suggestive proverb: *"He is not escaped who drags his chain!"* Gibbon tells of one of the Roman emperors who was brought from prison to the palace, and who sat for some hours on the throne with his fetters on his limbs. Thousands of those whom God has brought out of prison are in much the same condition. They are in the palace, but they carry about with them vestiges of the prison-life. They have escaped from the tyrant's custody, but they are not yet completely free; for as the grim jailer hears the rattle of the links sin has forged, and sees some of his fetters upon the soul, he still exercises his power, and indulges the hope that he may one day seize and entirely enslave his former captives. So long as we fail to perceive and claim deliverance from the power of indwelling sin through the wondrous Cross, we may give occasional evidence of our kingship, but we shall give unmistakable proof of our servitude.

Our message is one of complete deliverance. We believe that our regal honors are not a fiction, as they must have seemed to the king Gibbon tells of, but a glorious reality; and so we sing of Him who *"breaks the power* of *cancelled* sin," and of a Cross that effects a "double cure." The soul that dares, on the warrant of God's word, to claim identification with Christ in His death, resurrection, and enthronement, proves what it is to be a king in Christ Jesus; to such even the devils are subject, and the principalities and powers of darkness are made to feel the regal power of those who, clad in the armor of God, are more than conquerors through Him who shows His love to them by indwelling them. Charles Wesley sang of those who "hugged their chains." There are some who do this still; but there are many others, thank God, who hate them, and who long to lose every link that binds them to the conquered enemy.

The Cross of Christ not only enforces holiness, but makes holiness possible. Conybeare gives a striking translation of Galatians 2:20: "I am crucified with Christ; it is no more I that live, but Christ is living in me; and my outward life which still remains, I live in the faith of the Son of God, who loved me and gave Himself for me." Here we have both the exterior and the interior Cross. There is a great difference between realizing, "On that Cross He was crucified *for* me," and "On that Cross I am crucified *with* Him." The one aspect brings us deliverance from sin's condemnation, the other from sin's power. We first discover the Cross as coming between God and ourselves. That is its substitutionary or judicial aspect. In it Christ must ever be alone; into that circle none can enter; when He trod that winepress there was none with Him.

But there is an aspect of the Cross in the passage quoted which is not vicarious. "I am crucified *with* Christ; it is no more I that live, but Christ is living in me." Here we see the Cross coming between us and our sinful nature, and these words bring us face to face with a crucifixion which is experimental, for Christ does not vicariously deliver His followers from indwelling sin. It is a crucifixion which is inwrought by the power of the Holy Ghost, solely on our compliance with clearly defined conditions. The one is an outward, the other is an inward Calvary, the one is "the complement of the other, and their true union is their perfection."

The death of Christ was not only an atonement for sin, but a triumph over sin. By faith we see our sins not only on His head for our pardon, but under His feet for our deliverance. Multitudes who glory in the outward Cross know nothing of that inward crucifixion which it has also made possible, whereby they are delivered from the power of self and sin, the world, the flesh, and the devil. This they do *not* know, "that their old man was crucified with Him, that the body of sin might be done away, so that they should no longer be in bondage to sin" (Rom. 6:6).

There must be conformity between Christ and the members of His mystical body. How incongruous it is for a holy Christ to be leading a company of unholy Christians; or a cross-bearing Christ, a band of self-indulgent Christians, whose hearts are often towards Egypt, and who shrink from the least suffering and self-denial! It is only they who have truly followed Him, having known the meaning of this inward Cross, who will "have boldness, and not shrink with shame before Him at His coming."

Why hesitate, therefore, to bear the Cross by which you may gain the crown? In the Cross is salvation, in the Cross is life, in the Cross is safety from enemies; in the Cross is that peace which the world cannot give, in the Cross is courage, in the Cross is joy; in the Cross is the sum of all virtues, in the Cross the perfection of holiness. There is no salvation for the soul, no hope of eternal life in anything else. The Cross is the beginning and the end; and all who would live, must first die; there is no other way to life and to real inward peace but the way of the Cross.[1]

In times of persecution, those who had an experimental knowledge of this inward crucifixion were able to suffer the most terrible outward inflictions without shrinking or fear, while many of those who knew nothing of this interior Calvary abjured the truth to save their lives. Many instances are on record of such who afterwards—when they had learned to tread this royal road—came forward of their own accord and gave up their bodies to fire and death.

How much light this neglect of inward dying throws also on the doleful, shadowed death-beds of unsanctified Christians! When we have learned the blessedness of dying with Him, both to the flesh with its affections and lusts, and to the deceitful world, we shall know nothing in our last hours of the pains of death which those experience whose carnal hearts cling to carnal things. With an actual knowledge of inward death, we shall face that death which can only touch the outward, without any fear, and as cheerfully put off the body as we put off our clothes. We fear the great death so little, because, for Christ's sake, we have loved death with Him so well.

In physical crucifixion there were three stages. The criminal was first arraigned, found guilty, sentenced to death, and in many cases visited with marks of hatred and contempt. Then he was nailed to the cross, and finally he died. These three stages illustrate the experience of this inward crucifixion. First the old nature must be arraigned and sentenced, for it is not likely that the old Adam will be executed until,

by us, he is condemned to die. Then this enemy, which is both God's
and ours, must be given over into the hands of the only executioner,
the Holy Spirit. He will not undertake this work without our consent
and co-operation. "If *ye* through the Spirit do make to die the deeds of
the body, ye shall live" (Rom. 8:13).

"The law of death in our sinful members is only another form
of the law of life in Christ. It is the same Spirit who both killeth and
quickeneth. Though it is said most expressly that *we* crucify the flesh,
it is not said that *we* put it to death, and 'destroy the body of sin.' That
is the sole work of the Divine Spirit. It is His breath which withers the
fruits of evil in our nature; it is His condemning word that blights the
tree of evil in us unto its root. He will watch the expiring enemy within
us, ready to inflict upon it the last stroke that shall dispatch it finally.
We must not doubt that He will finish the work He has begun in us.
Crucifixion is not death; but it is unto death, and death is supposed to
be its result. If we do our part, and spare not our affections and lusts;
if we keep the sinning Adam in us crucified, and watch, and pray, and
wait in fervent expectation, we shall 'see the end.' And we shall see it
in this life, for there is no work of sanctification beyond the grave; and
surely there is no necessary connection between the death of the body
of sin and the death of the physical body. The Holy Ghost, we may
hope, will cry over our crucified flesh, with all its affections and lusts,
stilled and extinguished for ever. It is finished."[2]

The way of the Cross is certainly the way of death. The stoning
among the Hebrews, the guillotine of the French, the gallows of the
English, and the cross of the old Roman times, as instruments of capi-
tal punishment, all mean death. If at the outset of this Calvary experience we listen to the voices of the tempters, and withdraw the nails,
we cannot expect to know this real inward death; but if we have had a
vision of the loathsomeness of the old Adam nature, and of its power
to prevent the incoming and consequent outflowing of the risen life of
Jesus, we shall refuse for a moment to listen to its pleadings to be allowed to come down from the Cross and so save itself.

The Jews were not content with blows and buffetings and scourg-
ings; these were but the forerunners of death, and we may well beware
of attempting to "run with the hare and hunt with the hounds," or, in

other language, to make a pretence of inward crucifixion while at the same time we are secretly parleying with the enemy. We shall not parley if we resolutely remember that to do so is to prolong the life of "the old man," and so defeat the purpose of Jesus Christ, who was manifested not to buffet or maim but to "destroy the works of the devil," and only by that destruction can we know what real marriage union with Jesus means.

Hence it follows that our shrinking from the way of the Cross, and our fainting on that way, even when we have begun to tread it, arise from ignorance of the blessedness to which this pathway leads. The most joyous moment in the life of the bride ought to be the moment when she loses her own name and self-dependence at the marriage-altar, taking her husband's name instead of her own, and merges her life in his; and the most blissful moment in our life ought to be that in which we, by taking up our cross, renounce our right to self-ownership, and begin to reckon ourselves dead to self, to sin, and to the world, through the Cross of Jesus Christ.

> Oh, sacred union with the Perfect Mind,
> Transcendent bliss, which Thou alone canst give;
> How blest are they this Pearl of Price who find,
> And dead to earth, have learnt in Thee to live.

> Thus in Thine arms of love, O God, I lie,
> Lost, and for ever lost to all but Thee.
> My happy soul, since it hath learnt to die,
> Hath found new life in Thine Infinity.

> Go then, and learn this lesson of the Cross,
> And tread the way that saints and prophets trod:
> Who, counting life and self and all things loss,
> Have found in inward death the life of God.

That which is contrary to the world, and crucifies to the world, that is the Cross. The Cross hath this power and nothing else; and so there is nothing else to glory in. The flesh lusteth against the Spirit, and the Spirit against the flesh, and these are contrary one to the other. Mind here is the Cross: the Spirit which is contrary to the flesh, which mortifies the flesh, through the obedience whereof the flesh is crucified. "If ye through the Spirit mortify the deeds of the body, ye shall live." Whatsoever is of and in the Spirit is contrary to the flesh. The light of the Spirit is contrary to the darkness of the flesh. The holiness of the Spirit is contrary to the unholiness of the flesh. The life of the Spirit is contrary to the life (or rather death) that is in sin. The power of the Spirit is contrary to the power that is in Satan and in his kingdom. The wisdom of God is contrary and a foolish thing to the wisdom of man. Yea, the new creature which springs from God's Holy Spirit is contrary and death to the old.

—Isaac Pennington

CHAPTER 8

# The Victims of the Cross

O that the fire from heaven might fall,
Our sins its ready victims find,
Seize on our sins, and burn up all,
Nor leave the least remains behind!

WE have already pointed out that the Cross means death. It *may* mean a suffering, lingering, protracted death; there may be many convulsive struggles, but sooner or later death will follow continuous crucifixion, for it was always ignominious, violent, and effective. We use the word "continuous" advisedly, for they cannot expect a speedy end who, at the solicitations of the victim, withdraw the nails and renew its lease of life. This playing at the crucifixion of the flesh, with its passions and lusts, explains the unsatisfactory experience of multitudes, who by this means frustrate the grace of God.

God designs us to share the life of the risen Christ in all its heavenly beauty. We can only do this on the conditions so clearly revealed in His word, conditions which so completely harmonize with His character and working. What are they? "We were buried therefore with Him through baptism into death: that like as Christ was raised from the dead through the glory of the Father, so we also might walk in newness of life. For if we have become united with Him by the likeness of His death, we shall be also by the likeness of His resurrection; *knowing this,* that our old man was crucified with Him, that the body of sin might be destroyed, that so we should no longer be in bondage to sin; for He that hath died is justified from sin" (Rom. 6:4-7).

The principal thing for us to know is that "our old man" has been crucified with Christ, that he is one of the victims of the Cross. A few expositions of the terms employed in these verses may be of value here. Dr. David Brown, in his admirable handbook on this Epistle, says "'our old man' means 'our old selves,' all that we were in our old

47

unregenerate state before union with Christ. By 'the body of sin' *the whole principle of sin* in our fallen nature is meant—its most intellectual and spiritual, equally with its lower and more corporeal, features." The word rendered "destroyed," he reminds us, is a favorite one with Paul, used only once by any other New Testament writer, but twenty-five times by him. A reference to some of the passages in which it is so used may be helpful: 1 Cor. 6:13; 15:24, 26; 2 Cor. 3:7, 11, 13, 14; Eph. 2:15; 2 Thess. 2:8. The common-sense uses of this same Greek word, though variously translated in these passages, points to one conclusion and to one only.

Marcus Rainsford says: "By our 'old man' the apostle means our natural self, with all its principles and motives, its outgoings, actions, corruptions, and belongings; not as God made, but as sin and Satan and self have marred it. The old Adam never changes; no medicine can heal the disease, no ointment can mollify the corruption; it can only be got rid of by death."

Dean Alford defines our "old man" as our former self-personality before our new birth—opposed to the "new man" or "new creature." He says, moreover, "that as the death of Christ was by crucifixion, the apostle uses the same expression of our death to our former sinful self, which is not only put to death by virtue of, but also in the likeness of Christ's death—*as signal, as entire, as much a cutting off and putting to shame and pain.*" When it is remembered that Christ's was no fictitious execution, that He *really* died; that when the soldier thrust in his spear there was no lingering life to respond, it will be seen how complete is the purchased and promised deliverance from the plague of sin, which a great preacher has called "a foul, slimy protrusion into God's universe."

This, then, is the victim, whether it be called "the body of sin," or "the flesh," or "the carnal mind," or "the sin that dwelleth in me," or "the old man." It may have many names, it has but one cure, and that is death. It is unmitigated enmity to God, "The carnal mind is enmity against God" (Rom. 8:7). It is hateful to God, He can take no pleasure in any part of that nature which is under the curse, however pleasing and attractive it may be to man: "They that are in the flesh cannot please God" (verse 8). It is unimprovable, incorrigible, incurable. Cultured, educated and encouraged, or discouraged and threatened, its nature remains unchangeable. "It is not subject to the law of God, neither indeed can be" (verse 7). There remains then no remedy but that which God has provided—condemnation, crucifixion, death.

The Scriptures speak of the *seed* of the flesh, the *will* of the flesh, the *wisdom* of the flesh, the *purposes* of the flesh, the *confidence* of the flesh, the *filthiness* of the flesh, the *workings* of the flesh, the *warring* of the flesh, the *glorying* of the flesh.

All man's powers, reasonings, emotions, and will are under the power of the flesh. Whatever the fleshly mind may devise or plan, however fair its show may be, and however much men may glory in it, has no value in the sight of God. The flesh, with its thinking and willing and effort, is a victim for the Cross. We see the necessity of deliverance from what are commonly called the sins of the flesh, but how seldom do we include our powers to reason and think and plan. Alas! we often have confidence in these, and we are woefully discouraged because the Spirit does not prosper what the flesh has planned. Is not our worship of God often in the flesh? Are not plans and devices resorted to for obtaining money for the empty treasury of the Church, which bear upon their very surface the marks of the flesh, and which are so displeasing to God, that the workings of His Spirit are well-nigh quenched? It is little short of mockery, in many instances, to ask God's blessing on what our own heart tells us is the planning and working of the flesh, and which under the most beautiful and attractive guise can never be anything but offensive to Him.

Our natural life, and all the faculties with which it is endowed, must be sacrificed, immolated, renounced. Otherwise, after having flourished for a moment, with more or less of satisfaction, it perishes and withers for ever. This law applies to a pure being and to his lawful tastes. All that is not given to God by an act of voluntary immolation bears within it the germ of death.[1]

There is a subtle temptation, as in the case of Saul, to destroy the worthless and keep alive the best; in other words, to destroy the gross and spare the refined manifestations of evil. But when we claim to have fulfilled the commandment of the Lord, the searching question comes to many of us with the same terrible power, as it must have come to the disobedient king: "What meaneth then this bleating of the sheep in mine ears; and the lowing of the oxen, which I hear?"

That which is utterly destroyed can neither low nor bleat. It means then, nothing less than death to every doomed thing. Death to vanity, pride, covetousness, ambition, temper, impatience, fear, doubt, natural virtues, and natural affections; anything and everything that appertains to the old man, and which must be put off ere we can put on the new.

Have we consented to the nailing of this victim to the Cross? If we have, deliverance is certain, for the flesh received its death-stroke on Calvary. "Sin is smitten with the lightning of His anger. What was then accomplished in principle when 'One died for all,' is realized in point of fact when faith makes His death ours, and its virtue passes into the soul. The scene of the Cross is inwardly rehearsed. The wounds which pierced the Redeemer's flesh and spirit now pierce our consciences. It is a veritable crucifixion, through which the soul enters into communion with its risen Saviour, and learns to live His life. Nor is its sanctification complete till it is conformed unto His death (Phil. 3:10). So with all his train of 'passions and lusts,' the 'old man' is fastened and nailed down upon the new interior Calvary, set up in each penitent and believing heart. The flesh has no right to exist a single hour. *De jure* it is dead—dead in the reckoning of faith, and die it must in all who are of Christ Jesus."[2]

I think that this world, at its prime and perfection, when it is come to the top of its excellency and to the bloom, might be bought with a halfpenny; and that it would scarce weigh the worth of a drink of water. There is nothing better than to esteem it our crucified idol (that is, dead and slain), as Paul did. Then let pleasures be crucified, and court and honor be crucified. And since the apostle saith that the world is crucified to him, we may put this world to the hanged man's doom, and to the gallows: and who will give much for a hanged man? As little should we give for a hanged and crucified world. Yet fools are pulling it off the gallows and contending for it.

—Samuel Rutherford

O Lord, seek us, O Lord, find us in Thy patient care;
Be Thy love before, behind us, round us, everywhere:
Lest the god of this world blind us, lest he speak us fair,
Lest he forge a chain to bind us, lest he bait a snare.
Turn not from us, call to mind us, find, embrace us, bear;
Be Thy love before, behind us, round us, everywhere.

—Christina Rossetti

# CHAPTER 9

# The World and the Cross

Whatever passes as a cloud between
The mental eye of faith and things unseen,
Causing that brighter world to disappear,
Or seem less lovely, or its hope less dear,
*That is our world,* our idol, though it bear
Affection's impress, or devotion's air.

THE Galatian Epistle has been called the Crucifixion Epistle. In chapter 2:20, Paul says that his old self was crucified with Christ; in chapter 5:24, he tells us that his "flesh with its passions and lusts" had been nailed to the Cross; and now in chapter 6:14, he says that the world is crucified to him, and he is crucified to the world.

We read of "the spirit of the world" (1 Cor. 2:12), of "the fashion of the world" (1 Cor. 7:31), of the course of this world (Eph. 2:2), and of the prince of this world (John 14:30). We are told that the world is passing away, and that if we love it and the things that are in it, the love of the Father is not in us (1 John 2:15-17). Jesus prepared His disciples for its hatred, and told them this would prove they were not of it, for the world cannot hate itself (John 15:18, 19). He further teaches them that if they testify of it, as He ever did, that its works are evil, the world will hate them as it hated Him (John 7:7). Despite the inveterate hatred of the world, Christ's disciples are not to be afraid, for He tells them that He has overcome it (John 16:33); and His servant John assures those to whom he wrote, that "greater is He that is in them, than he that is in the world" (1 John 4:4); that whatsoever is born of God overcometh the world; and that this is the victory that overcometh, even their faith in its conqueror, Jesus the Son of God (1 John 5:4, 5).

What then is this world, which in the estimation of Paul was nothing better than a crucified felon? For be it remembered when we speak of the Cross, that in the early days of Christianity, none of those beautiful associations with which we are familiar had gathered round it. To us it is not only suggestive of a fact, but it is also a memorial of nearly two thousand years of history. The love and admiration with which we are familiar were unknown to the apostle. In his day it was the sign and symbol of ignominy, and far more odious and suggestive than the word gallows is to us. "There is, indeed," as one has said, "no word among us that is significant of the deep and acknowledged and universal detestation that belonged to the Cross."

The world "consists of those who are attached to sensible objects, and who place in them their sole happiness; who have a horror of poverty, suffering, and humiliation, and who look upon such things as real evils from which they must flee, and against which they must protect themselves at any cost; who, on the contrary, have the greatest regard for riches, pleasures, and honors; who consider these things as real and solid good; who desire them and pursue them with extreme eagerness, without caring what means they use to obtain them; who fight with one another over the goods of this life; who envy one another, and try to take from each other what they have not themselves; who only value another person, or despise him, in proportion as he possesses or does not possess these perishable goods. In one word, who found upon the acquisition and enjoyment of temporal things all their principles, all their code of morality, and the entire plan of their conduct."[1]

It is any form of life or government—political, educational, social, or religious—which does not place God pre-eminently first. To quote the language of Dr. Dale: To be worldly is "to permit the higher law to which we owe allegiance, the glories and terrors of that invisible universe which is revealed to faith, our transcendent relations to the Father of spirits through Christ Jesus our Lord, to be overborne by inferior interests, and by the opinion and practices of those in whom the life of God does not dwell. It is to regulate our life by public opinion instead of by religious principle, to do as others do without inquiring *why* they do it; to follow the crowd without inquiring where exactly they are going."[2]

Strongly do we recommend the readers of these pages to ponder Faber's searching and powerful description of the world in his *Creator and Creature*. He says: "The world is not altogether matter, nor yet altogether spirit. It is not man only, nor Satan only, nor is it exactly sin. It is an infection, an inspiration, an atmosphere, a life, a coloring matter, a pageantry, a fashion, a taste, a witchery. None of these names suit it, and all of them suit it. Its power over the human creation is terrific, its presence ubiquitous, its deceitfulness incredible. We are living in it, breathing it, acting under its influence, being cheated by its appearances, and unwarily admitting its principles."[3]

The world has its own prince, its own court, its own council, its own laws, its own principles, its own maxims, its own literature. It is the counterfeit of the Church of God, and the devil's principal weapon for lowering and poisoning the heavenly life in the individual and in the Church, and for antagonizing and destroying the work of the Holy Spirit. It is in our pulpits, choirs, and pews. It is all the more seductive because it makes an exterior profession of Christianity, and with infinite cleverness seeks to reconcile its own evil maxims with the doctrines of Christianity. It is far more to be dreaded than the undisguised attacks of the devil, for he urges his victims to glaring positive breaches of the Divine commands. The passions of the flesh in a similar manner impel to such sins as bulk prominently in the eyes of men, and startle them by their iniquity; but the spirit of the world fastens itself in diabolical subtlety upon those who pride themselves upon their spirituality and devotion, and who consider themselves so free from its hateful presence that they are offended if for a moment it is suggested that they are under its power. This is its great triumph, and when we laugh to scorn the suggestion that Madame Bubble will ever ensnare us in her toils, we are already among her dupes.

St. Paul was once among her victims. He counted the pride of birth and religion, worldly honor, wealth and pleasure, with the good opinion of men, to be gain; but in the light of the Cross his eyes had been opened to see the world's true character, and what things were once gain he now counted loss for Christ. Instead of looking to it for happiness, courting its smiles, and dreading its frowns, he regarded it as a condemned malefactor nailed to the Cross. Its wealth, honours, and pleasures could not seduce him, nor all its forces of hostility terrify him into a renunciation, or even concealment of one of the doctrines of the Cross (Gal. 6:12).

To him it would be as absurd as for a person to forfeit the favor of a much-loved sovereign who had every right to his affections and allegiance by seeking to secure a favorable glance from the eye of a worthless felon expiring on a cross. The same kind of horror that filled the mind of the Jew at the thought of a crucified malefactor, filled Paul's heart as he saw the snare into which the Galatian Christians were in danger of falling, that of making the object of God's curse the object of their regard and consideration.

The Cross had revealed to him such sources of enjoyment, and the crucified and risen Lord had so taken possession of Paul's entire being, as to lead him to say: "Yea doubtless, I count all things but loss for the excellency of the knowledge of Christ Jesus my Lord: for whom I have suffered the loss of all things, and do count them but dung, that I may win Christ, and be found in Him, not having mine own righteousness, which is of the law, but that which is through the faith of Christ, the righteousness which is of God by faith; that I may know Him, and the power of His resurrection, and the fellowship of His sufferings, being made conformable unto His death; if by any means I might attain unto the resurrection of the dead" (Phil. 3:8-11).

Just what the world was to St. Paul—an object of malediction with which he could have no connection, no association, no relationship—he was to the men of the world. He was to them an object of contempt, aversion, and hatred. He and his brethren were made a spectacle unto the world, and to angels and to men. "We are fools," said he, "for Christ's sake, but ye are wise in Christ: we are weak, but ye are strong: ye have glory, but we have dishonor. Even unto this present hour we both hunger, and thirst, and are naked, and are buffeted, and have no certain dwelling-place; and we toil, working with our own hands: being reviled, we bless; being persecuted, we endure: being defamed, we intreat: we are made as the filth of the world, the offscouring of all things even until now" (1 Cor. 4:10-13).

What is our relationship to the world, and what is its attitude towards ourselves? By these questions the thoughts of many hearts will be revealed. Some of us read, years ago, of a mountain of loadstone which drew by its tremendous power of attraction every piece of iron that was brought within the range of its influence. Ships at sea, passing near the shore of that land where the mountain was, felt its force on their anchors and chains and bars. At first their approach to the mountain was scarcely perceptible. There was a declining from their course, which excited very little apprehension. But the attraction gradually became stronger, until, with ever-increasing velocity, the vessel was drawn closer. Then the very bolts and nails started from the vessel's beams and planks, and fastened themselves on the sides of the mountain, the vessel, of course, falling to pieces and becoming a total wreck.

This legend may aptly illustrate our own peril, as it certainly illustrates the peril of the Church today; and the time has come when, with no uncertain sound, warning voices should be lifted up throughout the land, and compromise and concession with the world be absolutely prohibited in every shape and form.

"All that is in the world, the lust of the flesh, and the lust of the eyes, and the vainglory of life, is not of the Father, but is of the world. And the world passeth away, and the lust thereof: but he that doeth the will of God abideth for ever" (1 John 2:16, 17). By the first of these definitions of worldliness—the lust of the flesh—we understand the bodily appetites out of order or in excess. Until we have learned to crucify the flesh with its passions and lusts, or in other words to claim their sanctification, we shall find it impossible to bring them within the limits of God's appointment and law. Our first aim must be to achieve through faith victory over this inward world; over every propensity and appetite that sin has rendered inordinate and rebellious. These are refined lusts of the flesh—a fondness for luxuries, and an unwillingness to forego them. Tauler forcefully says: "As the old serpent laid low our first parents through gluttony, so his weapons are easily turned aside through soberness. We ought to take food in the same way as medicine, with such moderation and discretion, that it may help us to serve God; and with such gratitude, that at each single morsel praise may rebound to our Creator."

Then there is the "lust of the flesh" in the form of softness and self-indulgence. The unwillingness to endure hardness as good soldiers of Jesus Christ. The day's work is over, the boots are laid aside, and the slippered feet are put to the fire. How do we take any disturbance of our ease? How do we treat our self-denying Lord, when, in the guise of some poor widow or homeless wanderer, He comes to our door and asks for sympathy, or for food or clothing?

The "lust of the eyes." Think over the grim catalogue of Old Testament saints, and of New Testament saints too, who have fallen through the lust of the eyes. Let us not gratify this desire in any measure in even glancing at the poisoned pictures, and the poisoned literature which are thrust upon us today, and which are utterly unworthy of admission into Christian homes. It is a thousand times better to keep the heart pure, to have "nothing between," even though it means ignorance of a book over which the world has, for a few brief days, gone mad.

The lust of the eyes also points to the universal sin of insisting on something visible and tangible, of depending on the creature rather than on the Creator, instead of having the spirit of Moses who "endured as seeing Him who is invisible." How many unlike the man who, when called of God, went out, "not knowing whither he went," are always longing to *see* their way. We may live where the things that are unseen shall be the *most real* to us, and where we shall know that even our afflictions "work for us a far more exceeding and eternal weight of glory, while we *look* not at the things which are seen, but at the things which are unseen" (2 Cor. 4:18).

We may be comparatively free from the lust of the flesh and the lust of the eyes, and yet under the power of the world in this third aspect in which St. John regards it. "The vainglory of life" is the pomp and pride that exults in itself and does not give the glory to God. It is the heart fastening upon tangible objects, wealth, respect, and homage from without. There are scores of plans devised solely to foster these sinful propensities, some coarse and some so refined that there is about them the outline of beauty, the harmony of color and sound, the gracefulness of movement, the charm of sympathy: but in them all God would be such an intrusion, His presence would be so unwelcome, that they are immediately branded, beautiful though they be, as "not of the Father but the world." This is the true touchstone in our choice of food, dress, reading, and recreation; in all our buying and selling; in all our planning even for God's work. *Is this the will of God?* "The world passeth away. . . he that doeth the will of God abideth."

How afraid many are to brave the frown of others, when duties to which they are called comes into conflict with what the world calls etiquette! We must be saved from the desire to be thought well of by unsanctified Christians, who think far more of the maxims of society than they do of Christ, then we shall be the true courtiers, having learned how to deport ourselves in the school of grace. They only are God's gentlemen and gentlewomen who have claimed this complete deliverance from the spirit of the world.

When some terrible epidemic is raging, it is the constitution that is debilitated that takes the contagion. The healthy man is possessed of a vitality that enables him to walk through the streets where disease is rioting, and throw off the disease germs by the power of an abundant physical life. Worldliness only flourishes when the vitality of the Church is low, and as the Church is composed of units, when the vitality of *the individual* is low. The strong, exuberant overflowing life of Christ is our only safeguard, and the only secret of victory.

By appropriating first the victory of the Cross and then Christ's mighty resurrection-life, we shall be able to keep ourselves *unspotted* from the world. The religion of Jesus Christ knows nothing of bringing down her standards to suit the spirit of the age. It does not say to the business man whose surroundings are peculiarly trying: "Your case is one of peculiar difficulty, and I will waive part of my demands." It says to every man, though the atmosphere in which he lives is impregnated with this enervating poison, though he is surrounded with men whose ways are as crooked and tricky as the Adversary can make them, "Be separate!" "Touch not the unclean thing!" "Keep yourself *unspotted* from the world!"

A pilgrim once, so runs an ancient tale,
Old, worn, and spent, crept down a shadowed vale,
On either hand rose mountains bleak and high;
Chill was the gusty air, and dark the sky;
The path was rugged, and his feet were bare;
His faded cheek was seamed by pain and care;
His heavy eyes upon the ground were cast,
And every step seemed feebler than the last.

The valley ended where a naked rock
Rose sheer from earth to heaven, as if to mock
The pilgrim who had crept that toilsome way;
But while his dim and weary eyes essay
To find an outlet in the mountain side,
A ponderous sculptured door he spied,
And, tottering toward it with fast failing breath,
Above the portal read, "THE GATE OF DEATH."

He could not stay his feet that led thereto;
It yielded to his touch, and, passing through,
He came into a world all bright and fair;
Blue were the heavens, and balmy was the air;
And lo! the blood of youth was in his veins,
And he was clad in robes that held no stains
Of his long pilgrimage. Amazed, he turned;
Behold! a golden door behind him burned
In that fair sunlight, and his wondering eyes,
Now lusterful and clear as those new skies,
Free from the mists of age, of care, and strife,
Above the portal read, "THE GATE OF LIFE."

# CHAPTER 10

# The Gate of the Cross

SIR Noel Paton's beautiful picture, "Death the Gate of Life," has a significance other than that which seems to have been in the mind of the artist. The weary knight, wounded in his conflict with evil, has passed through the Valley of the Shadow of Death, and kneels in deep humility at the entrance of the world of light and life. He has put off his helmet with the crest of falcon wings and peacock's feathers—emblems of worldly ambition and pride. The belt and sword which are cast aside, and the armor which is falling off, indicate the renunciation of his own strength. The overblown hemlock, rank weeds, and withered branches on this side of the veil speak of sin's deadly poison and of disappointed hopes, while the white lilies and wild roses on the other side tell of the purity and joy which blossom there. The permanence of the life he is entering is indicated by a clear and steadfast star which shines in the sky, while the waning moon on the horizon typifies the mutability and evanescence of the life he is leaving behind.

All this symbolism applies as accurately to the spiritual as to the physical death. To attempt to conquer our sinful nature by doing battle against it is weary work, as many of us know. And while men age and even die in the strife with evil, sin never dies of old age. True, it changes its character, a new viceroy takes the place of the old one, but the government remains the same. At the transition point from one age of human life to another, a certain form of sin has to declare itself vanquished, but it is a victory over one of the outposts of sin, rather than over the tyrant in the citadel. Men have greatly rejoiced, for example, that the habit of intemperance has been conquered in their life, but that peculiarly abhorrent form of vice has often been succeeded by another, less abhorrent, perhaps, but none the less deadly. The capture of an advanced guard of sin has only challenged a new movement on the part of the enemy, and the slave of intemperance has become, all unconsciously, the slave of covetousness.

Well is it for us, if, like the knight in the picture, baffled, wounded, and weary after years of unsuccessful conflict, our pride conquered, and our own strength renounced, we are found kneeling at the door of that world which can only be entered through death-union with Jesus Christ. For when we come to a condition of utter bankruptcy, and deeply conscious of our poverty and powerlessness, cry out in abject despair, "O wretched man that I am, who shall deliver me?" we are at the threshold of deliverance. It will not be long before we begin to sing the victorious song: "There is therefore now no condemnation to them that are in Christ Jesus. For the law of the Spirit of life in Christ Jesus hath made me free from the law of sin and death" (Rom. 8:1, 2).

In giving an account of the terms proposed by Diabolus for the surrender of Mansoul, made through his ambassador Mr. Loth-to-Stoop, Bunyan brings home the intense anxiety of Satan to retain some hold upon Mansoul. "Then Mr. Loth-to-Stoop said again, 'Sir, behold the condescension of my master! He says he will be content *if he may but have some place assigned to him in Mansoul as a place to live in privately,* and you shall be lord of all the rest!' Then said Emmanuel, *'All* that the Father giveth Me shall come to Me, and of all that He giveth Me, I will lose nothing, no, not a hoof or a hair. I will not, therefore, grant him, no, not the least corner in Mansoul to dwell in. I will have it all to Myself.'" And blessed for ever be His name, for His gracious purpose and promise!

But it is only on the conditions we have sought to explain and enforce in the preceding chapters that He can have us all to Himself. There can be no revocation of the decree, "the soul that sinneth it shall die." We have to choose whether in union with the first Adam it shall be our own death, with the darkness and awful separation from God which it involves; or whether by our identification with the second Adam, it shall be death in *His* death and life in *His* life: "Because we thus judge, that One died for all, therefore all died; and He died for all, that they which live should no longer live unto themselves, but unto Him who for their sakes died and rose again" (2 Cor. 5:15).

"Our separation from sin is the result of His death. We may therefore overleap the ages and say, on that Cross my old life of sin came to an end: the nails which pierced His sacred hands and feet destroyed my old self. Christ and we were separated from sin by the same mysterious death; and therefore we are dead with Christ."[1] . . . "As we look back to Christ's death upon the Cross, and remember that in the moment in which He bowed His head He escaped completely from the enemies to whose assault, for our sakes, He had exposed Himself, we venture to believe that we are sharers of that deliverance, that upon His Cross we have ourselves escaped from the dominion of sin; and we also venture to believe that by faith and in Christ we already share the triumph of our risen Lord over all the enemies of Him and of us. Our faith is realized in actual experience. Henceforth His Cross stands between us and our sins: and through His empty grave we enter a life of victory."[2]

The poetical parable at the commencement of this chapter is no fantasy of the brain. Fellowship with Jesus in His death and risen life admits the believer, as many can testify, into a bright world where the heavens are blue and the air balmy. A world in which the inhabitants have learned the secret of perpetual youth; where they wear stainless robes; where the luster comes back to the eyes, and the mists of age and care and strife have forever passed away.

This is the unchanging law of the Christian life, for "the only way out of any world where we are is by death." It is a law which meets us at the very beginning of life in Christ, and as we walk in the light of God we shall have continuous discoveries of wealthy places, entrance into which is invariably through death, or in other words through ceasing to have fellowship with certain forms of life.

If you examined a dead leaf-stalk through a microscope, you would find that the old channel is silted up by a barrier invisible to the naked eye. On last year's leaf the plant has shut the door, condemning it to decay, and soon without further effort the stalk loosens, the winds of God play around it, and it falls away. The Cross of Christ shuts off the life of sin. "Our old man is crucified with Him, that the body of sin might be destroyed, that henceforth we should not serve sin: for he that is dead is freed from sin" (Rom. 6:6). Like the silted-up channel, the Cross stands a blessed invisible barrier between us and sinning as we "reckon" it there: that is, hold it there by faith and will. The sap—the will—the "ego" withdraws from the former existence, its aims and desires, and sends them into the new. And the first hour that the sap begins to withdraw, and the leaf-stalk begins to silt up, the leaf's fate is sealed.[3] But the sap which is withdrawn from the old is freely given for the nourishment of the new, and is only withdrawn for this purpose, for the gate of the Cross is ever the gate of life.

There is only one place where you can graft a branch upon a tree; it is where both the graft and the tree have been cut and the life is flowing out. But let there be close contact between them—for the smallest filament of wrapping round the graft will prevent the life of the tree from flowing into it—and what is the result? The little slip becomes a partaker of the strength and beauty of the stem, and as it bears leaf and fruit it seems to say: "I live, nevertheless not I, but the tree liveth in me, and the life I now live in foliage and fruit, I live by faith in the shaft of the tree." So to both graft and tree the gate of the cross is the gate of life.

A solitary grain of wheat will still "abide alone,"
    Unless 'tis placed beneath the soil to die—its beauty gone.
Then as it sinks from human sight, will kindly mother-earth,
    With forces all unseen, prepare the seed for its new birth;

Will pierce the outer husk, and free the imprisoned life within,
    So, that in all its loveliness the fresh growth may begin.
And in due time, above the ground, the green blade shall appear,
    And afterwards the ear, and then the full corn in the ear.

O wondrous parable of grace, teaching God's truth to me!
    My soul is like that grain of wheat: and e'er it fruitful be,
It must be yielded unto death, the self-life must be slain,
    And in the dark and silent ground my spirit must remain,

Till torn and bruised by discipline and tribulation drear,
    Sent by the loving Father's hand, the self shall disappear.
Then shall arise in silent strength the spirit-life within,
    Till soon it shall be manifest that I am "free from sin."

And as I daily "grow in grace," my life shall fruitful be,
    No longer "it abides alone," 'tis glorious, full and free.
O Lord! I yield myself to Thee to work in me Thy will,
    No more I'll dread my Father's hand, but trust Thee, and be still.
                             —A. M. P.

# CHAPTER 11

# The Fruit of the Cross

"VERILY, verily, I say unto you, Except a corn of , wheat fall into the ground and die, it abideth alone: but if it die, it bringeth forth much fruit" (John 12:24).

That we are here brought face to face with a truth of exceptional importance and significance is evident from the formula, "Verily, verily," with which our Saviour prefaces this statement. The truth which lies beneath the surface of this beautiful sentence may not be instantly perceived, it may, moreover, be repugnant to *our* conception of life and service—but this renders it only the more necessary that it should be pressed upon our attention.

Augustine reminds us that this "Verily, verily," is not the language of friend to friend; it rather indicates that we know so little of Christ's mind, and have so little confidence in Him, that His oath and bond are required by us before we can believe Him. Does not this language also reveal to us a Teacher, who bears with our slowness and ignorance, who deigns to meet us where we are, and who uses such words to arrest our attention as are needed by our dull intellect and unresponsive heart? May He not speak to my heart and thine, dear reader, in vain.

There is but one path to the blessedness which opens before us here. Abundant fruitfulness; the life which is life indeed; fellowship with Christ in service, and fellowship with Christ in glory, are all attained by death to self. The key to the wonderful life which is outlined here is: "EXCEPT IT DIE." Death is the gate of life; self-oblation is the law of self-preservation, and self-preservation is the law of self-destruction.

Two conditions of being are possible, either of which must constitute our character—love or self. Love seeks its life outside itself; self seeks its life in itself. Love, in order to possess, sacrifices selfishness; while self, in order to possess, keeps itself and sacrifices love.

The law which the great Teacher here illustrates from the vegetable kingdom, that self-sacrifice is the condition of all life, is a law universal in its application. It obtains throughout the physical universe, and "nothing truly lives or fulfils its true function, save as a part of the great whole, and in so far as it ministers to the welfare and advance of the whole. All things minister to and help each other—even sun, moon, and stars. All things give out life, or give up life and power, to quicken and cherish life in other forms; earth, water, and heat ministering to the life of the plant, the plant dying that it may minister to the life of bird and beast, bird and beast dying that they may minister to the life of man."

> "Life everywhere replaces death,
> In earth, and sea, and sky;
> And that the rose may breathe its breath,
> Some living thing must die."

To the Greeks peculiar difficulties were presented to the reception of the Saviour's teaching into their intellect and heart. For five centuries the Greeks had marched at the head of humanity. The whole world gathered round the torch of Greek genius. Their rich and flexible language, fashioned into the most perfect vehicle of thought, had become almost universal. Yet their failure in the regeneration of society was so conspicuous, that though the highest state of intellectual culture of which human nature is capable in its sinful state was attained prior to the Incarnation, their wise men were as though they had never been. Hence St. Paul asks, "Where is the wise? where is the scribe? where is the disputer of this world? hath not God made foolish the wisdom of this world?" (1 Cor. 1:20). So far as the moral and spiritual regeneration of mankind was concerned, these philosophers, thinkers, writers, and orators had left no trace of their existence, and men were halting between a superstition which believed everything, and a scepticism which believed nothing.

How is this failure to be accounted for? Their master-words were *self-culture* and *self-enjoyment.* This was, according to the Greeks, the supreme aim, the chief good of human life. The gods of Olympus were represented as beings who lived only to enjoy themselves, and who, when they came to earth, came only for the sake of pleasant adventure, or selfish amusement, caring nothing for the sins and sorrows of humanity. And the character of the gods was reflected in their Grecian votaries. Their highest conceptions of life was enjoyment of the senses, the intellect, and the imagination. And this was the life they loved and cherished.

Christ calls upon them to substitute self-oblation for self-culture, and self-sacrifice for self-gratification. In other words, He asks them to reverse the whole bent of their thought and conduct, and to set before themselves a conception of life diametrically opposed to that which they for centuries had held. As Godet says: "This saying included the judgment of Hellenism; for what was Greek civilization but human life cultivated from the view-point of *enjoyment* and withdrawn from the law of *sacrifice.*"

We cannot state too emphatically, in these days when self-sacrifice is so little understood, that it is the very salt of the Christian character, and that without self-sacrifice the Christian life is salt without the savor. It is the test by which, above every other test, a man may know what reality there is in his Christianity. And we halt over the elements and alphabet of the life divine, until we have learned to hate the self-life, and, renouncing it, have "laid hold on the life which is life indeed."

These are days of marvelous religious activity; but think of the disproportion between activity and achievement! Are there not multitudes of Christian workers who have grown so accustomed to failure that they have almost ceased to expect success? Surely with so much preaching and teaching, with so much Bible circulation and tract distribution, we ought not only to be holding our ground, but to be making inroads upon the kingdom of darkness. Yet we are not nearly keeping pace with the increasing population of the world, and today there are more millions sitting in darkness and in the shadow of death than ever there were.

One explanation of the fact that results are so often scanty and meager, or not real and abiding, lies here, *the initial step to fruitful service has not been taken.* Either through ignorance or unwillingness, the vast majority of those who profess to be fellow-workers with God in the regeneration of the world have never definitely hated and renounced the self-life, and it is because they are so much alive to self that they are so little alive to God.

Many, in their eagerness to succeed, are continually crying to God for the gift of spiritual power. But God cannot fulfill their desire, for He is a jealous God, and will not give His glory to another; and to trust men and women with spiritual power who are full of self-assertion would only be to feed their vanity and promote their self-idolization and love of self-display.

It is narrated of the great sculptor, Michael Angelo, that when at work he wore over his forehead, fastened on his artist's cap, a lighted candle, *in order that no shadow of himself* might fall on his work! It was a beautiful custom, and spoke more eloquently than, perchance, the sculptor knew, for the shadows that fall upon our work, how often do they fall from ourselves!

Is it so in your case, my reader? Are you, Baruch-like, seeking great things for yourself? Are *you* sensitive to the approbation or censure of men; elated when praised, disheartened when blamed? Do *you* consult your natural tastes and feelings in your work, missing the footsteps of Him who pleased not Himself? Do *you* shrink from the work that is disagreeable, that is unseen of men, and that carries with it no outward recompense? Verily, verily, I say unto you, you have your reward, but it is not the reward of gathering fruit unto life eternal.

It is said that properly ripened seeds, if placed in certain conditions, are capable of retaining their growing power indefinitely; not merely for a few years, not merely for a few centuries, but for thousands of years—how long, indeed, no man, can say. The earthy crust of our planet appears to be stocked in every part with seeds that have been produced in years gone by scattered upon the surface, and subsequently covered up with soil. Whenever the ground is disturbed, either by the plough, or by the spade of the railway excavator, or for any purpose which causes its depths to be overturned, that portion which was many feet below being thrown to the surface, and exposed to the air, the sunbeams, and the moisture of dew and rain, immediately there springs up a crop of young plants, certainly not originating in seeds, only just then brought from neighboring fields, and as certainly from seeds that have been lying in the soil for ages.

But away there in the depths of the earth, though the seed retains its vitality, it abides alone. Note, it is only as the seed dies that it attracts to itself the carbon, the nitrogen, and the various salts that contribute to the nurture of the grain, and that lie in the earth unused and unproductive until a power comes into contact with them that brings them forth from their lurking-places. The latent life-germ needs the penetrating sunbeam and the warm rain of heaven, then decay and death begin, and out of decay and death spring life and beauty. What dormant powers, what Divine possibilities lie sleeping in human lives today! What talents and gifts are buried away in those depths! If men and women would only expose themselves to "the open sunshine of God's love," and throw open their hearts to the fertilizing dew of His Spirit, there would start into life latent forces, which, under the vitalizing power and guidance of the Holy Ghost, would fill hundreds of other lives with blessing, and their own with unspeakable joy.

"Except a corn of wheat *fall into the ground and die,* it abideth alone: but *if it die,* it bringeth forth much fruit." Let us follow, in imagination, that corn of wheat as it falls into the ground. Within its tiny husk is the farina or flower, and inside that a Divine secret, a life-germ, which the microscope cannot detect. It is full of latent life, and contains the germ of boundless harvests. But its dormant capabilities are only quickened, and that secret germ is only released by a rending asunder, a disintegration, a death.

The little seed surrenders itself to the forces of nature, which seize upon it and speedily destroy its shapeliness and beauty. Down there, beneath the red mould, God has His laboratory, and He carries on and completes that process of transmutation which is the most wonderful that takes place beneath the sun. As the dissolution takes place, the life-germ begins to feed on the farina till it is all consumed.

It is like a prisoner shut up in his cell with a cruse of water and a crust of bread, and when the water is consumed to the last drop, and the crust consumed to the last crumb, then it begins to burst its prison walls. The germ then divides into two. One, the plumule, tends upwards, the other, the radicle, tends downwards. The part that shoots downwards, seeks from the soil such particles as are required to build up its future life, and passes them on for the growth of the plant in the upper air. It lays all nature under contribution for its sustenance; from earth and sky it borrows materials of growth, and at length becomes a luxuriant corn laden with its fruitful ear.

"Now mark," says Rev. C. G. Moore—in a most suggestive article on this subject—"how much larger is the life which the corn of wheat can lay hold of in its new body. As to *receiving*, it at once has fellowship with all the resources of nature. Air, light, rain, dew, earth, all minister to its upbuilding and welfare. From all these in its former body it could take nothing. As to *giving*, too, what a change! For now it bringeth forth fruit, thirty-fold, sixty-fold, it may be a hundredfold." The spiritual application of this is so apparent, that every reader will be able to make it for himself.

Before the Son of God stooped to clothe Himself in human form—in order that He might become "obedient unto death, even the death of the Cross"—every element of power *(excepting self-sacrificing love)* had been tried and had ignominiously failed. But the Cross becomes a throne, and the crucified a conqueror; He who was lifted up from the earth is drawing all men unto Himself, and the measure of *our* drawing power is the measure of our self-emptied and Christ-possessed lives, for "except it die it abideth alone, but if it die it bringeth forth much fruit."

Have you ever heard of the aloe plant,
Far away in the sunny clime?
By a humble growth of a number of years
It reacheth its blooming time;
And then a wondrous bud at its crown
Breaks into a thousand flowers:
*But the Plant to the flower is a sacrifice,*
For it blooms but once, and in blooming dies.
And each and all of its thousand flowers,
As they drop in the blooming time,
Are infant plants that fasten their roots
In the place where they fall on the ground;
And fast as they fall from the dying stem
Grow lively and lovely around;
*So dying, it liveth a thousandfold*
*In the young that spring from the dead of the old.*

You have heard of Him whom the heavens adore,
Before whom the hosts of them fall;
How He left the choir and anthems above,
For earth, in its wailing and woes;
To suffer the pain, the shame of the Cross,
And die for the life of His foes!
He died, but His life, in numberless souls,
Lives on in the world anew.
His seed prevails and is filling the earth,
As the stars fill the sky above;
*He teaches to yield up the love of life*
*For the sake of the life of love;*
His death is our life—His life the world's glory,
And we are commanded to spread the glad story.

Life out of death—
Dear Master, is it spoken
    Of the life here, or in the better land?
Nay, wherefore wait? the vessel, marred and broken,
    Shall *now* be molded by the Potter's hand.

Life out of death—
Oh, wondrous resurrection!
    Seed sown in conscious weakness, raised in power;
Thy life lived out in days of toil and friction,
    "Not I, but Christ" in me—from hour to hour.

Life out of death—
A pilgrim path and lonely,
    Trodden by those who glory in the Cross;
They live in fellowship with "Jesus only,"
    And for His sake count earthly gain but loss.

Life out of death—
Blest mission to be ever
    Bearing the living water, brimming o'er,
With Life abundant from that clear, pure river,
    Telling that thirsty souls need thirst no more.
                    —M. C.

CHAPTER 12

# The Gains of the Cross

"HE that loveth his life shall lose it; and he that hateth his life in this world, shall keep it unto life eternal" (John 12:25). The word "life" here is expressed by two Greek terms having quite a different meaning. The one, as the margin of the Revised Bible suggests, might be translated "soul"; it is the Greek *psyche,* and stands for our lower, our soulish, or self-life; the second word refers to the higher, the divine life. If we love the lower life, if we listen to the philosophy of the world, which is *"Spare, thyself: the cross be far from thee,"* we lose, of necessity, the higher, the abundant life; for we cannot have, at one and the same time, what the world calls "life" and what Christ calls "life."

Mr. Spurgeon tells of a raw countryman, who brought his gun to the gunsmith for repairs. The latter is reported to have examined it, and finding it to be almost too far gone for repairing, said, "Your gun is in a very worn-out, ruinous, good-for-nothing condition, what sort of repairing do you want for it?" "Well," said the countryman, "I don't see as I can do with anything short of a new stock, lock, and barrel; that ought to set it up again." "Why," said the smith, "you had better have a new gun altogether." "Ah," was the reply, "I never thought of that: and it strikes me that's just what I do want, a new stock, lock, and barrel; why that's about equal to a new gun altogether, and that's what I'll have."

That is just the sort of repairing that man's nature requires. The old nature must be cast aside as a complete wreck, and good for nothing, and the man made a new creation in Christ Jesus. But willing as we may be to admit this truth, few lessons are harder to learn.

Christ's sacrifice utterly condemned me in my natural state. It was as if He said: "O Righteous Father, I offer up and renounce this man's impure soul, that it may die; and that My life may live and grow in him." Have I yet learned to hate, renounce, deny, and deliver over to

75

death, in the unity of my Lord's sacrifice, my condemned selfhood? Until I have, I shall never know the meaning of the words "If any man serve Me, let him follow Me," for we only follow Him by sharing in the spirit of His self-sacrifice. That may mean for us a way of humiliation and seeming defeat; but not in service that arrests widespread notice or excites the admiration of the multitude, do we always best serve Christ. Ours may be a baptism of sorrow and pain, for strait is the gate and narrow is the way that leadeth to this life, and few there be that find it.

The soulish life longs for ease, for indulgence, for display, for wealth, for position, for popularity, and it is recorded as one of the marks of the grievous times that characterize the last days, that "men shall be lovers of self, lovers of money, boastful, haughty. . . without self-control. . . puffed up, lovers of pleasure rather than lovers of God; holding a form of godliness, but having denied the power thereof" (2 Tim. 3:2-5, RV).

It has been remarked that all things thrive in proportion as they relate themselves to the world around them; in proportion as they surrender themselves to their environment. While the branches surrender their independence and lose themselves in the tree, they grow beautiful with leaf, and flower, and fruit; but as soon as they detach themselves from the general life, they begin to wither and rot, and men gather them into bundles and burn them. While the members surrender their individual life to the one life of the body, the rich blood courses through them, and they become strong and vigorous, but a severed member soon becomes a withered and shapeless thing. So the selfish man ethically destroys himself by selfishness. In proportion as we give we shall receive, and the power of perfect sacrifice is also the power of perfect life.[1]

The exclamation of Jesus in John 12:27 reminds us that not without pain and anguish does the dissolution of the self-life take place. "Now is my soul troubled; yet what shall I say? Father, *save* me from this hour. But for this cause came I unto this hour. Father, glorify Thy name." Here is a picture of the conflict which goes on in many lives between the higher and the lower natures, when God's call comes "to be united together with Christ by the likeness of His death" (Rom. 6:5, RV).

How many agencies God employs to bring us to an end of our self-life! "Think of the seed cast into the earth exposed to wintry winds; trodden under the feet of those who drive the rake and harrow over it; buried out of sight and left alone, as if cast out by God and man to endure the slow process of a daily dissolution, then melted by rains and heats until its form is marred, and it seems useless to either God or man." So in a variety of unexpected and unwelcome ways does God bring to destruction that which He has condemned to death. How strikingly this is illustrated in the case of Job! Yet all the despoiling forces, men and devils, friends and foes, were held in leash by the strong hand of Love, who, when His purposes were accomplished, said, "Thus far shalt thou go and no farther."

To cry out, "Save me from this hour!" to shrink and murmur, is only to disappoint God, to aggravate the evil, and to frustrate His purposes of grace. It is through the valley of the shadow of death, through the fiery way of trial, that we are brought into the wealthy place. It is God who directs the movements of the Sabeans and Chaldeans; it is He who permits the whirlwind to devastate and death to destroy, and our deliverance is not in fleeing from the marauding bands, but in saying, as Jesus did, "Father, glorify Thy name!" Whatever this means of severance and suffering, "Father, glorify Thy name!" and like our Master, we shall hear a voice which assures us, "I have both glorified it, and will glorify it again."

We shall do well to be on our guard against attempting to conquer self by any active resistance we can make to it by the powers of nature, for "nature can no more overcome or suppress itself, than wrath can heal wrath." Our very efforts to overcome it seem to give it new strength; self-love finds something to admire, even in the very attempts we make to conquer it. It will even take pride in what we mean to be acts of self-humiliation. There is no deliverance for us from this dread tyrant *but in God.* We are not skilful, or brave, or disinterested enough to wage this war alone. We must set ourselves against this foe which is His as well as ours, and while we strive in all things to work together with Him, we must trust Him to work for us and in us, till self shall die slain by God's own breath. As living, intelligent beings, we must yield to the inspiration of the power that kills and makes alive, for God does not work irresistibly as upon dead matter, but intellectually and spiritually as upon honest mind. Self being slain, his brood of gross affections will disappear; so that instead of the works of the flesh will appear the fruit of the Spirit (Gal. 5:19-24). "Instead of the thorn shall come up the fir tree, and instead of the brier the myrtle tree" (Isa. 55:13). Instead of the repulsive *I* life shall appear the beautiful Christ-life. "No longer I, but Christ."

Let us get these three truths firmly fixed in our mind. First, dying to self is the *one only way* to life in God. The end of self is the one condition of the promised blessing, and he that is not willing to die to things sinful, *yea, and to things lawful,* if they come between the spirit and God, cannot enter that world of light and joy and peace, provided on this side of heaven's gates, where thoughts and wishes, words and works, delivered from the perverting power of self—revolve round Jesus Christ, as the planets revolve around the central sun.

Secondly, the only cure for self is *death.* It is unreformable in its character, and immutable in its workings. It can no more change from evil to good than darkness can work itself into light, and therefore death to self is the one only way to life in God.

Thirdly, the only conqueror of self is Christ. It is the law of the Spirit of life in Christ Jesus that sets us free from the law of sin and of death (Rom. 8:2). The ruling monarch will never dethrone himself, but if we welcome the Christ of God into the temple where self has been enshrined, the hideous idol will fall before His word as Dagon fell before the ark.

As Andrew Murray says: "Self can never cast out self, even in the regenerate man. Praise God! the work has been done. The death of Jesus, once and for ever, is our death to self. And the gift of the Holy Spirit makes our very own the power of the death-life."

A word of warning is perhaps necessary, lest, actuated by some selfish aim, our self-sacrifice only becomes deeper self-seeking. It is not a bartering of a bad self for a better self, but a foregoing and utter renunciation of self for ever. "Whosoever will lose his life *for My sake,*" said Jesus, "shall find it."

Self-sacrifice for the sake of self-discipline is a delusion indeed; *it is nothing but self-culture;* the very life we profess to be seeking to overcome is actually being fed and strengthened by, what we think to be, blows struck at its very existence. Our self-sacrifice is utterly valueless unless it bears this stamp upon it, *"For My sake."*

As to the recompense of this self-renouncing life. What words can describe it! For a season the grave may seem to be dark and dreary; there may be a desertion and a loneliness which are hard to the flesh, but as suffering was the pathway which the Saviour trod in order to enter into His glory, so through this same experience is every son of man glorified, and God is glorified in him. As one has beautifully said: "Those who die with Christ are safe with Him. For His own life-guard of angels is about them, to watch and roll away the stone, that the dead may, in due time, rise again."

In all true sacrifice there is more of joy than sorrow. The whole life of God is just the outflowing of His love, and the sacrifice of Christ is simply the full revelation of that wondrous love. It is no pain, surely, to a lover to give himself and all he has to his beloved. Nay, "It is *more blessed to give* than to receive," and the richest, truest, and most lasting of all blessedness is the blessedness of self-giving. The stairway of self-oblation leads men ever upwards and onwards, from the life of Christ to the likeness of Christ, the fellowship of Christ, the throne of Christ, and the glory of Christ: "For to him that overcometh will I grant to sit with Me in My throne, even as I also overcame, and am set down with My Father on His throne."

> Measure thy life by loss instead of gain,
> Not by the wine drunk but by the wine poured forth;
> For love's strength standeth in life's sacrifice;
> And whoso suffers most hath most to give.

Look not for a true living strength, in the life of the *Me* and the *I*,
With nothing to love but its selfhood, and fearing to suffer and die.
As thou seekest the fruit from the seed-planted grain,
Seek life that is *living,* from life that is slain.

Then hasten to give it its death-blow, by nailing the *I* to the Cross;
And thou shalt find infinite treasure in what seemed nothing but loss;
For where, if the seed is not laid in the ground,
Shall the germ of the new resurrection be found?

The soul is the Lord's little garden, the *I,* is the seed that is there;
And He watches it while it is dying, and hath joy in the fruits it doth bear.
In the seed that is buried is hidden the power
Of the life-birth immortal, of fruit, and of flower.

'Tis hidden, and yet it is true; 'tis mystic, and yet it is plain;
A lesson, which none ever knew, but souls that are inwardly slain;
That God, from thy death, by His Spirit shall call
The life ever-living, the life ALL IN ALL.

—Professor T. C. Upham

# CHAPTER 13

# Beauty for Ashes

SOME years ago, on engineering a malarious district in South America, so many of the men were stricken down with sickness that the engineer resolved to destroy the luxuriant undergrowth of weeds, flowers, ferns, mosses, and lichens, by fire. The result was six months of continued burning and smoldering, until, to all appearance, the life-principle was eradicated from soil and subsoil. After two years of desolation and sterility, a little plant appeared, developing in due time a flower so rich in its loveliness, and so rare in its beauty, as to fill the beholder with amazement and admiration. It was submitted to floral experts for classification, but they knew of no class to which it belonged. They had never seen anything like it, and they were obliged to let it stand alone in its unique loveliness.

This aptly illustrates the spiritual desolation which precedes that death to the life of nature, and to the subtleties of our selfhood, to which we must come ere we know the risen life of Jesus in all its fullness and fruitfulness. To human eyes the life is rich in foliage, here are lovely mosses, there are wonderful lichens; but human eyes cannot detect the malaria of selfishness which God sees. It is no longer selfishness in its repulsive forms, but in its most deceitful and attractive dress. It may be described as consecrated selfishness, or selfishness for God.

Now it takes the form of impulsive and intense earnestness. Work is undertaken because it *seems* to be of God, but the will of God has not been sought, nor has His strength been put on, hence creaturely energy takes the place of Divine power. Now it takes the form of jealousy for God's glory, and a position of antagonism is taken to some project, which position says in unmistakable language: "Come and see *my* zeal for God;" but bitter criticisms are indulged, and uncharitable thoughts are cherished, which reveal only too clearly the malaria of a strong and subtle selfhood.

Or it takes the form of a craving for spiritual enjoyment. The finger is ever on the pulse of the emotions, and the soul is constantly inquiring "How do I *feel?*" So long as this emotional pulse beats strongly all is well, but if it grows faint and feeble, the soul is immediately plunged into the Slough of Despondency. This is particularly manifest in work for God. The guidance of the Spirit is honestly sought, and the spirit is cast upon Him for aid. If, however, after the work has been done, there should be an utter divestiture of emotional experience, the temptation of going back upon the guidance of the Spirit is indulged, and hours of anguish follow, because the tempter's lie is believed, that the wrong course was taken and the wrong message given. This anguish is greatly aggravated if some prized human opinion is adverse to what has been said or done; and the victim of these experiences not infrequently threatens, because self-love has been thus wounded, to abandon work for God altogether.

The purpose of God is to deliver His children from this life, which is still a mixed life, and full of vicissitudes and variations, and give in its place a life fixed and permanent, where the spirit, delivered from selfishness in every form, and in full union with the Divine will, rests solidly upon the great Center, and upon that alone. Do not let it be for a moment thought that we are minimizing or deprecating the experience that has been already attained. The soul has *true* life, but not *full* or *perfect* life; God is not yet that *"all in all"* which He longs to be, and He cannot and will not let us rest in *any* good which is outside Himself.

This experience is a painful one. It is nothing less than the hating and renouncing and losing (so that it will never be found again) of the life of nature, and the being filled with the life and fullness which is of God. (Note how, in the following passages, Christ insists on this: Matt. 16:25-27; Mark 8:35; Luke 9:24; 14:25-35; John 12:25.)

In the Life of Madame Guyon there is a striking description of the passage through this experience. In the year 1674, she entered into what she terms her state of *privation* or *desolation,* and continued in it, with but slight variations, for more than six years. Protracted and painful though her experience was, few have been better able than she to say: "So then death worketh in us, but life in you" (2 Cor. 4:12), for while she lived, and all through these two hundred years since she slept in Jesus, her personal knowledge of spiritual desolation and death has brought light and life to multitudes.

"I seemed to myself," she says, "cast down as it were from a *throne of enjoyment,* like Nebuchadnezzar to live among beasts—a very trying and deplorable state, when regarded independently of its relations, and yet exceedingly profitable to me in the end, in consequence of the use which Divine wisdom made of it." All *sensible* consolation vanished. God set in motion a train of circumstances which seemed to add fuel to the fire, until that to which she had clung with such tenacity, and delighted in with such exceeding delight, was nothing but a heap of ashes. But, as her biographer says, "God designed to make her His own, in the highest and fullest sense; He wished her to possess the true life, the life unmingled with any element which is not true; in other words, a life which flows directly and unceasingly from the Divine nature. And in order to do this, it became with Him, if we may so express it, a matter of necessity that He should take from her every inward support, separate and distinct from that of unmixed naked faith. She could love God's will, trying though it often was to her natural sensibilities, when it was sweetened with consolations; but the question now proposed to her was, whether she could love God's will when developing itself as the agent and minister of Divine providences which were to be received, endured, and rejoiced in, in all their bitterness, simply because they were from God?"

Describing this season of aridity and inward deprivation, she says: "Confused, like a criminal that dares not lift up his eyes, I looked upon the virtue of others with respect. I could see more or less of goodness in those around me, but in the obscurity and sorrow of my mind, I could seem to see nothing good, nothing favorable in myself. When others spoke a word of kindness, and especially if they happened to praise me, it gave a severe shock to my feelings, and I said in myself they little know my miseries; they little know the state from which I have fallen. And, on the contrary, when they spoke in terms of reproof and condemnation, I agreed to it as right and just."

Then she tells how nature sought to free herself from this abject condition, but could not find any way of escape. She was like the slain that lie in the grave; to all appearance cut off from God's hand and laid in the lowest pit, in dark places in the deeps. Shut up, she could not come forth, and she cried in her anguish: "Wilt Thou show wonders to the dead? shall they that are deceased arise and praise Thee? Shall Thy loving-kindness be declared in the grave? or Thy faithfulness in destruction? Shall Thy wonders be known in the dark? and Thy righteousness in the land of forgetfulness? But unto Thee, O Lord, have I cried" (Psalm 88, RV).

After nearly seven years of inward and outward desolation the darkness passed away, and the light of eternal glory settled upon her soul. Out of the ashes of the consumed selfhood God brought forth a life so novel and beautiful, that the Christians of the day in which she lived failed to classify it. It was so unlike anything they had ever experienced, heard, or read of, that they put her in prison for possessing it.

She learned to look back upon these years as the darkness of the grave that precedes the resurrection glory; the consuming to ashes that precedes the growth of never-fading flowers; the night of mourning that comes before the morning of joy; the spirit of heaviness that is worn before the garment of praise.

"It was on the 22nd of July, 1680, that happy day," says Madame Guyon, "that my soul was delivered from all its pains. On this day I was restored, as it were, to perfect life, and set wholly at liberty. I was no longer depressed, no longer borne down under the burden of sorrow. I had thought God lost, and lost for ever; but I found Him again. And He returned to me with unspeakable magnificence and purity. In a wonderful manner, difficult to explain, all that which had been taken from me was not only restored, but restored with increase and new advantages. In Thee, O my God, I found it all, and more than all! The peace which I now possessed was all holy, heavenly, inexpressible. What I had possessed some years before, in the period of my spiritual enjoyment, was consolation, peace—the *gift* of God rather than the Giver; but now, I was brought into such harmony with the will of God, whether that will was consoling or otherwise, that I might now be said to possess not merely consolation, but the GOD of consolation; not merely peace, but the God of peace. *One day of this happiness, which consisted in simple rest or harmony with God's will, whatever that will might be, was sufficient to counterbalance years of suffering.* Certainly it was not I, myself, who had fastened my soul to the Cross, and under the operations of a providence, just but inexorable, had drained, if I may so express it, the blood of the life of nature to the last drop. I did not understand it then; but I understood it *now.* It was the Lord that did it. It was God that destroyed me, that He might give me the true life."

Two observations will perhaps prevent misconception at this stage. First, the phrase, "the life of nature," is used of the natural life *without* the restoring and purifying grace of full sanctification. The life of nature is the opposite of the life of faith. The one is always seeking its own will and acting in independence of God, while the other seeks the will of God and makes Him the foundation of every action. The one looks to man's wisdom and man's strength, the other rejects all methods and instrumentalities which are dissociated from God. Augustine wisely says: "God is never the *destroyer* of nature, but He *ordereth* it and maketh it perfect."

It will be wise, in the second place, to say that this deep work of the Spirit *need* not be protracted over years, as in Madame Guyon's case. If utterly abandoned to God—determined to shrink from no discovery, however humbling, and no purging, however severe—the soul will only "*reach forth*" to the things that are before, ever "pressing towards the mark"; God will very quickly show forth the killing and quickening power of His Spirit.

To heaven approached a Sufi saint,
From groping in the darkness late,
And tapping timidly and faint,
Besought admission at God's gate.

Said God, "Who seeks to enter here?"
"'Tis I, dear Friend," the saint replied,
And, trembling much with hope and fear.
"If it be *thou,* without abide."

Sadly to earth the poor saint turned,
To bear the scourging of life's rods;
But aye his heart within him yearned
To mix and lose its love in God's.

He roamed alone through weary years,
By cruel men still scorned and mocked,
Until from faith's pure fire and tears
Again he rose, and modest knocked.

Asked God, "Who now is at the door?"
"It is *Thyself,* beloved Lord,"
Answered the saint; in doubt no more
Of an exceeding great reward.
                              —*Translated from the Persian*

# CHAPTER 14

# The Dying Life

WE have sought to show that *fullness* of life can only follow *reality* of death. If we shrink from laying the life of nature upon the altar of Christ's Cross, if the sense of desolation and apparent abandonment by God and man affrights us, we shall never reach the goal towards which the Holy Spirit has been leading us from the very commencement of the impartation of the life of God.

In one of his wonderful sermons, Tauler gives a powerful description of what he calls the three stages of the dying life, remarking that "in what measure a man dies to himself and grows out of himself, in the same measure does God, who is our life, enter into him."[1]

In the first stage, men are apt to taste little sweetness in loving God, save when they hope to enjoy something of His love; as for instance to escape hell and get to heaven. Such begin to die while they love themselves far too well. They desire that all men should be as they are, and whatever methods of avoiding sin they have practised, and still make use of by reason of their infirmity, they desire, nay demand, that everyone else should observe; and if any do not do so, they judge them, and murmur at them, and say that they pay no regard to religion.

Such men, who are standing on the lowest steps of a dying life, are very niggardly of their spiritual blessings towards their fellow-Christians; for they devote all their prayers and religious exercises to their own advantage; and if they pray or do any other kind act for others, they think it a great thing, and fancy they have done them a great service thereby. Their whole life is full of care, full of fear, full of toil and ignoble misery; for they see eternal life on the one side, and fear to lose it; and they see hell on the other, and fear to fall into it; and all their prayers and religious exercises cannot chase away their fear of hell, so long as they do not die unto themselves. They make long stories of what is of no consequence, and talk about their great difficulties and sufferings, as if they were grievously wronged; and they esteem their works, though small, to be highly meritorious, and that God owes them great honor and blessing in return. From this first step many, through unwillingness to go forward, fall back from the little they have attained, and plunge into folly and wickedness.

In the second stage, Tauler describes the experience we have referred to in the previous chapter. The soul can endure insult, contempt, and such like deaths, so long as he is sustained by a gracious sense of the Divine presence, but directly *that* is withdrawn, the man falls a prey to mistrust of God, fancying that God has forgotten him and is not willing to help him towards perfection. When the Lord shows him some kindness, he feels himself so rich as if he could never be poor, and thinks to enjoy the presence and favor of God (though as yet he is quite untried) just as if the Almighty were his own personal, special friend; and is ready to believe that our Lord is, so to speak, at his disposal to comfort him in adversity, and enrich him with all virtue. Seeing that such a man will be very apt to rely upon his imagined powers, and thus to fall grievously, seeing also that the best and ripest fruit is being lost, inasmuch as the man has not yet attained to that perfection to which our Lord desires to lead him, in due time our Lord withdraws from such a one all that He had revealed to him, because the man was too much occupied with himself, thinking about his own perfection, wisdom, holiness, and virtues.

Thus brought through poverty to dissatisfaction with himself, he humbly acknowledges that he has neither wisdom nor worthiness. He was wont to desire and thirst after the reputation of holiness, like a meadow after the dew of heaven. He fancied that men's praise of him had proceeded altogether from real goodness and by God's ordination, and had wandered so far from self-knowledge as not to see that he was in himself unsound from head to foot; he fancied that he was really as he stood in man's opinion, and knew nothing to the contrary.

In order that he may learn to know himself, our Lord suffers him to fall into unspiritual temptations such as he never experienced in those past days in which he fancied himself very good and spiritually minded. Out of mercy God deprives him of all understanding, and overclouds all the light in which he walked aforetime, and so hedges him in with the thorns of an anguished conscience, that he thinks nothing else but that he is cast from the light of God's countenance; and he moans greatly, and often with many tears exclaims: "O my God, why hast Thou cast me off, and why go I thus mourning all the days of my pilgrimage!"

When he finds himself thus, from the crown of his head to the sole of his foot, unlike God and at variance with Him, he is filled with such a sense of his own unworthiness that he can hardly abide himself; and then he thinks many miserable things about himself from passages of Holy Scripture, and sheds many tears in the sense of his sinfulness, till he is weighed down to the earth with the pressure of God's hand, and exclaims: "My sins have taken hold upon me, that I am not able to look up!" He asks the heavens why they have become as brass, and the earth wherefore she is as iron, and beseeches the very stones to have compassion on his woes.

So God leads the soul through these exercises and operations of His hand as through fire and water by turns, until the workings of self-sufficiency are driven out from all the secret corners of the spirit, and the man henceforward is so utterly ashamed of himself, and so casts himself off, that he can nevermore ascribe any greatness to himself, but thoroughly perceives all his own weakness in which he now is, and always has been. Whatever he does or desires to do, or whatever good thing may be said of him, he does not take it to his own credit, for he knows not how to say anything else of himself, but that he is full of all manner of infirmity. Then he has reached the end of this second stage; and he who has arrived at this point is not far from the threshold of great mercies, by which he shall enter into the bride-chamber of Christ. Then, when the day of his death shall come, he shall be brought in by the Bridegroom with great rejoicing.

Little trees do not strike their roots deep into the earth, and therefore they cannot stand long; but the great trees, which are intended to endure long upon the earth, these strike their roots deep, and spread them out wide into the soil. So it is with those who are great upon earth; they must needs, through many a struggle and death, die unto themselves before all the self-sufficiency of their heart can be broken down, and they can be surely and firmly rooted for ever in humility. It does, however, happen sometimes that the Holy Spirit finds easier ways than those of which we have spoken, whereby He brings such souls to Himself.

The third stage of this dying life is reached only by those who, with unflagging diligence and ceaseless desire, are ever pressing forward to perfection. In this stage, there is a mingling of sorrow and of joy. An overwhelming sorrow in the sense of the unspeakable wrong done to God by His creatures, and especially by the inconsistent disciples of Jesus Christ. An overwhelming gladness in the assurance that he is now to be filled with all the joys that the human nature of Christ possessed.

To this state a man cannot attain except he unite his will with God, with an entire renunciation and perfect denial of himself, and all selfish love of himself, and delights in having his own will overmastered and quenched by the shedding abroad in his heart of the Holy Spirit in the love of God, so that it *seems* as though the Holy Spirit Himself were the man's will and love, and he were nothing and willed nothing on his own account. Yea, even the kingdom of heaven he shall desire for God's sake and God's glory, because Christ hath earned it in order to supply his needs, and chooseth to bestow it on him as one of His sons.

"Dying together" with Jesus,
    *This* is the end of strife!
"Buried together" with Jesus,
    *This* is the gate of life!
"Quickened together" with Jesus,
    By the touch of God's mighty breath;
"Risen together" with Jesus,
    Where is thy sting, O Death?

"Living together" with Jesus,
    Walking this earth with God;
Telling Him all we are doing,
    Casting on Him every load.
Living His life for others,
    Seeking alone His will,
Resting beneath His shadow,
    With a heart ever glad and still.

"Seated together" with Jesus,
    In the "heavenly place" of love;
Love, unequalled—unending,
    In the heart of the Father above.
"Seated together" with Jesus,
    To *live* out the love of God,
And so win this world unloving,
    By His love so deep and so broad.
            —BESSIE PORTER

CHAPTER 15

# The Risen Life

THE Cross of Christ, as St. Paul preached it, contains all the elements of moral regeneration and of spiritual life. He never gloried in the Cross as a narrow technicality, but as illustrating, and, we might even say, incarnating the length and breadth, and depth and height of the love of God. To the apostle, the Cross of Christ started from the Incarnation on the one side, and led up to the Ascension and Enthronement on the other.

"If we have become united with Him by the likeness of His death, *we shall be also* by the likeness of His resurrection" (Rom. 6:5). According to the completeness of our union with Him in the one, will be the completeness of our union with Him in the other. Unbelief repudiates what Christ has done; for, as Dr. Pfleiderer says: "The objective reconciliation effected in Christ's death can after all benefit actually, in their own personal consciousness, only those who know and acknowledge it, and feel themselves in their solidarity with Christ to be so much one with Him as to be able to appropriate inwardly His death and celestial life, and to live over again His life and death; those only, in a word, who truly *believe* in Christ."[1] Paul's faith fully endorsed all that Christ had done as His representative. He had joined His Saviour on the Cross, he had gone down with Him into the grave, and because He had come forth from the tomb Paul had come forth too, for "in this appropriation of the death and rising of the Lord Jesus there are three stages, corresponding to the Friday, Saturday, and Sunday of Eastertide. 'Christ died for our sins; He was buried; He rose again the third day:' so, by consequence, 'I am crucified with Christ; no longer do I live; Christ liveth in me.'"[2]

Burial is the seal and certificate of death. Christ's interment in the rock-hewn sepulcher gave conclusive evidence of the reality of His death. His enemies said, "That is the end of another deception," while

His friends said, "We *trusted* that it had been He who should have redeemed Israel." The phrase "buried with Christ" denotes, then, the absoluteness of our death with Him, as a man who passes away is said to be dead and buried. The relatives and friends of a Hindu convert to Christianity, in order to show how completely they had cast him off, actually celebrated his funeral, and treated him, after this open display of his death, as if he really no longer existed.

The reckoning of faith which results in identification with Christ in His death may be at first a secret, and only known to God and ourselves, but it must not remain a secret. The average Roman of the period when this letter was written was accustomed to the amphitheater. He became, by the law of association, brutalized and ferocious to the last degree. Coming under the power of Christ, he died to the degradation and cruelty of the amphitheater, and because the fashions of the age were such that no follower of Christ could consent to them, he became dead to society, and of necessity the secret was soon out that he had joined the ranks of the despised Jesus. He was as much dead and buried to these things as if his body had been laid in the grave.

Just as we have all known what it is to turn away at last from the grave-side where the body of some loved one has been laid to rest; just as we have lingered to take the last look at the coffin, and have then come away with tear-dimmed eyes, feeling all was over, so they who are really dead and buried with Christ, think of that old natural self as having been wrapped in its winding-sheet, and buried in the dark grave with Christ's burial. The old habits, the old besetments, the old sins are as completely past and gone as is the dead body lying in yonder grave. So Tersteegen sings:

> Dead and crucified with Thee, passed beyond my doom;
> Sin and law for ever silenced in Thy tomb.
>
> Passed beyond the mighty curse, dead, from sin set free;
> Not for Thee earth's joy and music, not for me.
>
> Dead, the sinner past and gone, not the sin alone;
> Living, where Thou art in glory on the throne.

And now let us dwell on some of the features of this risen life. It introduces us into a new world; "it puts an end to all our former opinions, notions, and tempers; it opens new senses in us, and makes us see high to be low, and low to be high; wisdom to be foolishness, and foolishness wisdom; it makes prosperity and adversity, praise and dispraise, to be equally nothing."

This risen life is marked by *perpetuity*. There are animals which hibernate, and for all practical purposes are dead for a season: for a season they abandon their haunts and habits, but when the warmth of spring penetrates their burying-place, there is a revival of their old instincts. So there are those whose death is so unreal, that the abandonment of sin is only temporary, and while they think themselves dead, the soul of sin lives on underneath the lethargic surface, and when the cause of its insensibility has passed away, returns with strengthened life to all its old habits and ways. Such was not the death and risen life of Jesus. This may mean, and ought to mean the entrance into an experience where there need be no relapses into sin. "The death that He died, He died unto sin *once for all;* but the life that He liveth, He liveth unto God. *Even so,* reckon ye also yourselves to be dead unto sin, but alive unto God in Jesus Christ" (Rom. 6:10, 11). Let us emphasize that *once for all.* There should be no relapses into the realm of death. Sin is the tomb of the soul, and if we have risen, let us be sure we do not return to it. There must be no periodic visits to the sepulcher; we must die unto sin *once for all,* and as Jesus never returned to the sepulcher after He left it, so let us resolve never to return; so that it may be said of us with regard to the old associations, habits, and indulgences, as it was said of our Lord, "he is not here, he is risen."

Again, this risen life is marked by *activity.* We are to be *"alive* unto God." To be alive to anything is to take a keen, intense interest in it. The tradesman does not simply want as assistants those who will keep their hands out of his till, but those who are so alive to his interests as to make them their own.

The deviation of a ship's compass from the true magnetic meridian is caused by the near presence of iron. This disturbing influence must be neutralized, or the compass becomes worthless. The deviation of the soul from its God-ward course is caused by the presence of sin in the nature, and as long as sin remains uncrucified, we shall be alive to its influence, and therefore not truly alive to God. There are disturbing forces at work in the unsanctified soul which prevent the hearing of God's voice and the doing of God's will.

When Paul was charged by the Corinthians with caprice and fickleness (2 Cor. 1), he denied the charge on the ground that he was a *spiritual* Christian. "The things that I purpose, do I purpose according to the flesh, that with me there should be the yea, yea, and the nay, nay?" Paul's inner being was once like an undisciplined mob, the voices of self-interest, ambition, and of policy being all heard in turn, but it was not so now. He claims to be "established in Christ," and to be "anointed," which "means freedom from all selfish and personal wishes, deliverance from those passions whose name is legion, and power to sit at the feet of Jesus clothed and in our right mind! A man who is free from the manifold motives of self-will moves like the sun—steady, majestic, with no variableness, neither shadow of turning. His course can be calculated. Paul claimed that because he was in Christ he *could not* be tricky, or manoeuvre, or do underhand things."

Fullness of life will certainly result in activity and intensity. The man who is really united to Jesus has his own life destroyed out of him and the life of Christ communicated to him. The life which Christ reproduces in us cannot be idle, unsympathetic, cold, parsimonious, or seclusive from men's joys and sorrows. That life will unfold itself, where there is nothing to hinder it, as naturally as the vine produces grapes. "I confess," says Madame Guyon, "I do not understand the resurrection state of certain Christians, who profess to have attained it, and who yet remain all their lives powerless and destitute: for here the soul takes up a true life. The actions of a raised man are the actions of life; and if the soul remains lifeless, I say that it may be dead or buried but not risen. A risen soul should be able to perform without difficulty all the actions which it has performed in the past, only they would be done in God. Those who believe themselves to be risen with Christ, and who are nevertheless stunted in their spiritual growth and incapable of devotion—I say, they do not possess a resurrection life, for there everything is restored to the soul a hundred-fold."

There ought to be no room for the objection that this life of perfect union with a risen Saviour leads to an introspective and largely meditative life. It is difficult to detect anything that is introspective in the lives of George Fox and John Wesley, for example, after they had entered into resurrection life. Their lives were filled with holy, self-forgetful activities. Like their Master, they were anointed with the Holy Ghost and with power, and they went about doing good, and healing all that were oppressed with the devil, for God was with them (Acts 10:38). This risen life is not the imitation of a splendid model, but the indwelling of a living Person. The Christ-life is only the outward development of the Christ nature; the life manifesting itself after its kind. Personal and abiding union with Him makes it as easy for the believer to do Christlike works, as for the branch to bear the luscious fruit when it is in unhindered fellowship with the vine. "He that abideth in Me, *and I in him,* the same beareth much fruit: for apart from Me ye can do nothing" (John 15:5). "Verily, verily, I say unto *you,* He that believeth on Me, the works that I do shall he do also; and greater works than these shall he do; because I go unto the Father" (John 14:12).

This risen life is characterized by *newness.* We are raised with Jesus that we may walk henceforth in "newness of life," and "if any man is *in* Christ, he is a new creation: old things have passed away; behold, *all things have become new*" (2 Cor. 5:17). God is not the God of the dead, but of the *living,* and this new life is the crowning joy of union with the risen Jesus. We blunder when we make the mystic grave the goal; for we are the children of the resurrection, and the goal is life so unspeakably energizing, fresh, free, and joyous, as that words fail to describe its blessedness. This new life is so heavenly in its character, that it makes its possessor responsive to everything with which it has affinity, both in heaven and earth. Who can enjoy the sounds and sights of this fair world—which are but "the drapery of the robe in which the Invisible has clothed Himself"—like the man who is living in the perpetual enjoyment of God's fresh life? Having been brought into perfect harmony with God, he appreciates everything in its true and Divine relation—*all in God, and God in all.* He sings as only a child of the resurrection can sing:

Heaven above is softer blue,
Earth around is sweeter green,
Something lives in every hue,
Christless eyes have never seen;
Birds with gladder songs o'erflow,
Flowers with deeper beauties shine,
Since I know as *now* I know,
I am His, and He is mine.

In everything which is really of God there is a singular freshness and novelty. The crucified and quickened believer has a new heart and a new spirit; by a new and living way he enters into the holiest place; he walks in a life which is new, every moment; his delight is in obeying the new commandment; his mercies are new every morning; with a new tongue he sings the new song; and bearing a new name, he is destined to reign with his Lord in that kingdom of which God says, "Behold, I make all things new!"

This risen life is once more a *hidden* life. "Ye are dead, and your life is hid with Christ in God" (Col. 3:3). "He that is joined unto the Lord is one spirit" (1 Cor. 6:17). "I am not ashamed to say that I believe there is an experience of union with the Lord which is rightly characterized as pantheistic, in which God has met all the needs of the soul, and has become the indwelling power of the human spirit; that the man who is thus united to God moves as God moves, and acts as the Lord wills him to act in the body and in the circumstances in which he is placed. Christ can be all in all in the nineteenth century as well as in the first, and we do not need to think Him less than He wishes to be to those who trust in Him."[3]

It was from this fact that the early disciples derived much of their strength and courage. Thus Paul wrote: "Knowing that He which raised up the Lord Jesus shall raise up us also with Jesus, and shall present us with you: for which cause we faint not: for though our outward man is decaying, yet our inward man is renewed day by day" (2 Cor. 4:14, 16). The calm of God's presence had settled down upon the man who wrote these words, and in nothing was he terrified by his adversaries; living his life "within the veil," he knew that in the very perfection of opposition (see Rom. 8:35-37) he would be more than conqueror through Him who loved him. The adversaries might rage, the storms might beat, the kings of the earth might set themselves against the Lord's anointed ones, but though the circumference was a whirl the center was at rest, and the secret was a life hidden with Christ, where no sharp arrow from the enemy's bow could penetrate, and where there was consequent "quietness and confidence for ever" (Isa. 32:17).

In one of the Perthshire valleys there is a tree which sprang up on the rocky side of a little brook, where there was no kindly soil in which it could spread its roots, or by which it could be nourished. For a long time it was stunted and unhealthy, but at length, by what may be called a wonderful vegetable instinct, it sent a fiber out across a narrow sheep bridge which was close beside it. Then fixing itself in the rich loam on the opposite bank of the streamlet, it began to draw sap and sustenance, and speedily became vigorous. What that tiny bridge was to the tree, the resurrection of Jesus is to the believer. If the roots of our life are in our Risen Lord, we shall not be stunted and unhealthy, as they must ever be who seek to find nourishment for their spiritual life in the unkindly soil of the world. "Thus saith the Lord, Cursed is the man that trusteth in man, and maketh flesh his arm, and whose heart departeth from the Lord: for he shall be like the heath in the desert, and shall not see when good cometh; but shall inhabit the parched places in the wilderness, a salt land and not inhabited. Blessed is the man that trusteth in the Lord, and whose trust the Lord is: for he shall be as a tree planted by the waters, and that spreadeth out her roots by the river, and shall not fear when heat cometh, but her leaf shall be green; and shall not be careful in the year of drought, neither shall cease from yielding fruit" (Jer. 17:5-8).

Tauler beautifully says: "As the loadstone draws the iron after itself, so doth Christ draw all hearts after Himself which have once been touched by Him; and as when the iron is impregnated with the energy of the loadstone that has touched it, it follows the stone uphill although that is contrary to its nature, and cannot rest in its own proper place, but strives to rise above itself on high; so all the souls which have been touched by this loadstone, Christ, can neither be chained down by joy nor grief, but are ever rising up to God out of themselves. They forget their own nature, and follow after the touch of God, and follow it the more easily and directly the more they are touched by God's finger."

True resurrection life is an *unchanging* life. The Aaronic priesthood was marked, as the writer to the Hebrews tells us, by intermittency and change. "They indeed have been made priests many in number, because that by death they are hindered from continuing: but He, because He abideth for ever, hath His priesthood unchangeable. Wherefore also He is able to save completely them that draw near unto God through Him, seeing He *ever liveth* to make intercession for them" (Heb. 7:23-25). The whole system was marked by change, weakness, and death. It could not effect anything that was abiding and permanent, much less that was eternal. And the inner life of the worshipper corresponded to the system; it was marked by fluctuation and decay. There was excuse for an intermittent spiritual life then, there is none now, because our Priest "ever liveth." The life He lives is one of irresistible strength and energy, and is indissoluble and indestructible in its character. It is a life that withstands victoriously the wear of time, the convulsions wrought by the progress of knowledge, and the severest assaults of hostile criticism. Just as the life in the power of which He ministers is unchangeable, so the life He ministers to all who are in perfect union with Him is a life that is unchangeable too. And because there is never a moment when His priestly action, His watchful care, His loving sympathy and succor, His working in us the power of an endless life are not in full operation, we may abide *for ever* in the life streams which flow from the throne of our Risen Lord through the power of the Holy Ghost, who is sent forth from the Father to be the bearer of this unchanging and abundant life to every soul that wills to receive it.[4]

There comes to us, if we will but appropriate it, moment by moment, through the indwelling of Christ's other Self, heavenly life, heavenly peace, heavenly joy, heavenly victory:

> All the life of heaven above,
> All the life of glorious love;

For "the kingdom of God is righteousness and peace and joy *in* the Holy Ghost." The intermittency which may have marked and marred our lives in the past, need therefore be our experience no more, and will be no more ours while "we walk in the light as He is in the light," and practically recognize the truth, "All my fresh springs are in Thee."

It follows from all that has been said that this risen life is characterized, lastly, by *complete and constant victory.* "Christ being raised from the dead, dieth no more; death no more hath dominion over Him" (Rom. 6:9). The death of Christ meant the conquest of the world, the flesh, and the devil. "He was crucified through weakness, yet He liveth through the power of God. For we also are weak in Him, but we shall live with Him through the power of God toward you" (2 Cor. 13:4). Christ's human body came at last to an end of all its capacities and resources, and He died of mortal weakness. We see Him bearing the burden of the world's sin, despised and rejected, a Man of sorrows and acquainted with grief, wounded for our transgressions, bruised for our iniquities; surrounded by taunting foes, scourged, buffeted, spit upon, bound upon the Cross of shame, then dying of a broken heart. "He was crucified through weakness, but He liveth through the power of God."

When Paul wants a concrete illustration of this power, he turns to the tomb of Jesus, and tells us that the flood-tide of resurrection power which invaded that lifeless form, that irresistible vital force which swept through that cold clay and renovated it until it was instinct with resurrection life and beauty in every part, is the power which is to usward who believe. And when, like that worn and exhausted body, our native powers are brought by the withering breath of the Holy Spirit to utter collapse, we are in the place where we may begin to live by the power of God; where He who lifted Jesus out of the grave, out of the earth into heaven, and then to the throne of God in heaven, will raise us up also with Him. The power that effected the one miracle is quite equal to the accomplishment of the other (Col. 2:12).

The victory of the head carries with it the victory of the body. The subordination of every force, whether hostile or friendly, carries also with it present victory and exaltation for every member of the true Church, "which is His body, the fullness of Him that filleth all in all" (Eph. 1:19-23).

Child of the Eternal Father,
    Bride of the Eternal Son,
Dwelling-place of God the Spirit
    Thus with Christ made ever one;
Dowered with joy beyond the angels
    Nearest to His throne,
They, the ministers attending
    His Beloved One:
Granted all my heart's desire,
    All things made my own;
Feared by all the powers of evil,
    Fearing God alone;
Walking with the Lord in glory
    Through the courts Divine,
Queen within the royal palace,
    Christ for ever mine;
Say, poor worldling, can it be,
That my heart should envy thee?
                    —GERHARD TERSTEEGEN

# CHAPTER 16

# Married to Another

"WHEREFORE, my brethren, ye also were made dead to the law through the body of Christ; that ye should be married to another, even to Him who was raised from the dead, that we might bring forth fruit unto God" (Rom. 7:4). Such is the language in which the apostle sets forth the blessedness of the risen life. In this seventh chapter he shows us what it is to be married to the law, set forth in the figurative capacity of a husband. The husband is holy and spiritual, righteous and good (verses 12-14), and demands perfect love to God and perfect love to man. This love is wanting owing to the wife's inability, her love being centered in self, and not in God. The husband is displeased, and threatens death if she does not obey. While the wife fully recognizes the reasonableness both of the requisition and the threatening, she finds herself unable—though she promises obedience again and again—to fulfill the requirements of her husband, the law.

If she only had the strength, and could render him the loving obedience he demands, her life might be one of unsullied happiness, for, as it has been said: "the law may be a very good husband for an unfallen angel, but it is a very unsatisfactory one for a fallen man, who is 'without strength,' and in whom there 'dwelleth no good thing.' Law presupposes strength, and indicates and rewards its right use: but 'power unto strengthless souls' it cannot give."

When this first husband is once offended, he will never again be reconciled. Should the wife expostulate, "But I wish to do your will;" he replies, "Speak not of wishes, but do it." But, says the wife, "I have done it in almost every particular;" he only answers, "Whoso shall keep the whole law, and yet offend in one point, is guilty of all." "May I not be forgiven?" asks the distressed wife; he answers, "There is no forgiveness in my nature;" "the soul that sinneth shall die;" "cursed is everyone that continueth not *in all things* that are written in My book to do them."

After vainly endeavoring to render the requisite obedience, and constantly crying out: "To *will* is present with me, but to *do* that which is good is not," the wife at last gives up in despair, and the penalty of her disobedience is about to be exacted when Christ appears. He reveres, honors, and loves the husband, and entirely approves of his requirements and the course he has taken. But while He condemns the wife, He pities her, and with deep benevolence loves her. He can do nothing to lower the sanctions of her husband's requirements; he must not only not be dishonored, but he must be magnified and made honorable. Christ pities the wife so much as to be willing to die for her; so, *by the body of Christ,* we become dead to the law. The holy and dishonored law had only one thing to give the unfaithful wife—*its curse,* and "Christ has redeemed us from the curse of the law, being made a curse for us." The curse of sin is *abandonment by God,* and on the Cross that curse, with all its unspeakable accompaniments, fell on the spotless soul of Jesus. Abhorred of men, forsaken of God, earth all hate, heaven all blackness, the curse that we had merited claimed Him as its victim, and by taking our place He has bought us for ever out of its power.

We have read of certain venomous animals which expire the moment they have deposited their sting and its mortal poison in the body of their victim. Thus there ensues a double death—that of the sufferer as well as the assailant. Under the law's awful curse, Jesus poured out His soul unto death; but at the same moment the law expended all its power as a judge and avenger over those who identify themselves with Christ. The handwriting of ordinances that was against us and contrary to us has become powerless since it was nailed to His Cross. It became from that moment *the receipt* of a discharged obligation. All the right and strength of condemnation which belonged to it were put forth on that Cross. Payment to the uttermost farthing was demanded, and payment to the uttermost farthing was made. The law has no more power over a dead subject than the husband has over a dead wife. The death of either contracting party frees both from their obligations, and the moment we choose to reckon ourselves to have died in Christ, that moment we pass from under the curse, and can sing: "There is now therefore no condemnation to me, for I am *in* Christ Jesus."

Freed from her union with the law in the death of her Deliverer, the wife is now free to marry again. Her Deliverer has risen from the dead, and on proposing marriage to her for whom He died, her heart is won, her selfishness is conquered, and with her whole soul she enters into a *love* relationship. She needs no stern and terrible legal sanctions to keep her from revolting from her husband's will; such is the union between her spirit and His, that love is law, and law is only love. Her second husband's requirements are fuller than the first, for He came into the world to fulfill the law, and He died and rose again, that married to Him we might fulfill it too; "that the requirements (see RV) of the law might be *fulfilled in us,* who walk not after the flesh, but the Spirit" (Rom. 8:4). The wife was too weak to obey her first husband, and he was too weak to render her any assistance; but now the Conqueror of sin, death, and hell is the Bridegroom of her soul. The law has become incarnate in Him who has won her heart, and "*His commandments are not grievous.*" Hence the bitter wail of inability and defeat of the seventh chapter—"To *will* is present, to *do* is not! O wretched one that I am, who shall deliver me?"—gives place to the triumphant paean of the eighth chapter: "The law of the Spirit of life in Christ Jesus has made me free from the law of sin and death!" "I am more than conqueror through Him that loveth me!" "If He is for me, who can be against me?"

The seventh chapter of Romans is largely the complaint of one married to the law, seeking by struggle and effort to obey his behests. The eighth chapter is the language of the soul's triumph when "married to another, even to Him who was raised from the dead." In union with Him there is no more *condemnation,* v. 1; no more *enslavement,* v. 2; no more *unrest,* v. 6; no more *death,* v. 10; no more *loneliness,* v. 10; no more *inability,* v. 11; no more *fear,* vv. 14, 15; no more *doubt,* v. 16; no more *poverty,* v. 17; no more *anxiety,* v. 28; no more *defeat,* v. 37; no more *separation,* v. 38.

Let us further see what this marriage union with Jesus involves. An earthly relationship, with which we are familiar, and with the conditions of which we are well acquainted, is used to shadow this wonderful heavenly relationship. When writing of it in his letter to the Ephesians, Paul said: "This is a great mystery" (Eph. 5:32). This, however, is clear,

God has purposes of love towards us which may well overwhelm us as we contemplate them. No such dignity is proposed for any other created being, and we are driven to the conclusion that human character, formed in full union with Jesus Christ, and by the unhindered operation of the Holy Spirit, may be, even here and now, a grander thing than can be found elsewhere in the universe. Our present position, as the betrothed of Jesus, is unique; our destiny as His bride is unique; and it is no matter for wonderment if the conditions of trial and training to which we are here subjected, to fit us for a position of such elevation and distinction, are also unique.

By this marriage of the soul to Jesus we become partakers of the Divine nature (2 Peter 1:4). "We are members of His body; being of His flesh, and of His bones" (Eph. 5:30). As the woman owed her natural being to the man, her source and head, so we owe our entire spiritual being to Christ, our source and head: and as the woman was one flesh with the man in this natural relation, so we, in our entire spiritual relation, spirit, soul, and body, are one with Christ. "For this cause shall a man leave father and mother, and shall be joined unto his wife, and the two shall be one flesh. Christ is here the man in the apostle's view, the Church is the woman. The saying applies to that past, present, and future which constitutes Christ's union to His bride, the Church. His leaving the Father's bosom, which is *past;* His gradual preparation of the union, which is *present;* His full consummation of it, which is *future.* We are as truly now one flesh with Him, as we shall be when heaven and earth shall ring with the joy of the nuptials."

Shall we be surprised if, with such a purpose, our heavenly Bridegroom should be jealous of the least complication of our lives, of the least diversion of our affections in any other direction! "Partakers of the Divine nature, having escaped the corruption that is in the world in lust." This corruption we must escape in union with Jesus in His death; for it is not in the elements which surround us, but in our own hearts; because there reign the vicious and wicked affections, whose source and root is denoted by the word lust. The world in which the corruption is, is in ourselves. It is in proportion as we escape this, and enter into the wondrous purpose of God, that we shall see how reasonable it is that He should have us all to Himself; and how He could not, with such a love, rest satisfied in anything short of this. This perfect union of nature with our Lord is, as Tauler says, "the dearest and most desired thing that God will have from man: then man will be always so disposed that God can work in him at all times without hindering, and therefore He also saith, 'My delight is with the children of men.'"

Someone has called attention to the three stages of love. At first the ruling thought of the soul is "My Beloved is mine, and I am His" (Songs 2:16). At this stage we think chiefly of Christ as ours, and so in some way for our pleasure. Then we come to "I am my Beloved's, and my Beloved is mine" (6:3). *His* ownership and possession take the first place in our thoughts. At last we come to "I am my Beloved's, and His desire is towards me" (7:10), where the word "mine" is altogether dropped, in the perfect assurance of love that to be His indeed, involves all.

The marriage of the soul to Jesus carries with it the *power to render obedience.* The wife of the second husband is just as much under obligation as she was in her former marriage. Nay, the obligation is far greater. Take one illustration only: the first husband said, "Thou shalt love the Lord thy God with all thy heart;" but the second says, "This is my commandment, that ye love one another, *as I have loved you,*" thus supplying herewith a new model for her love. What was previously an impossible task, becomes now a delightful privilege, for the very purpose of this union is contained in the Saviour's prayer: *"That the love wherewith Thou hast loved me, may be in them, and I in them."* "He is *in* His people that He may draw down to them the love of the Father, which flowed toward Him when He was separately present in this world; and He is in them, that He may perennially exhibit to His people the love He bears them. The vocation of every believer is this: to be a revelator of the love of Christ. The believer is an epistle of Christ—an epistle of His love."[1] So that what was impossible by a constraining principle from without, is delightfully possible by an impelling power from within. The second Husband therefore supplies a new motive as well as a new model, and to every call, His beloved may make answer: "The love of Christ constraineth me." She serves now not in the oldness of the letter which is Sinai, but in the newness of the Spirit, which is Pentecost.

Marriage to Jesus means also perpetual *fruitfulness.* We are "married to Him who was raised from the dead, that we might *bring forth fruit unto God."* In a familiar chapter in St. John's Gospel, the fruit of union to Christ is similarly set forth, only the figure there is a *vegetable,* as here a *conjugal* one. "Fruit unto death," as verse 5 tells us, is the outcome of living in the flesh; just as "fruit unto God" is the outcome of union with Jesus. *"Fruit"* is the spontaneous natural manifestation of the life within. The great question is, Are we in right relations to Jesus? Is our union with Him so complete, that every pore and artery of our being is open to receive the perpetual inflow of His life? If so, we need have no anxiety about fruit. If we take care of what we are, what we do will take care of itself.

Flowers that are bent on perfecting themselves by becoming double, end in barrenness. This mysterious union of our nature with Jesus means marvelous development; but it means also *reproduction,* for the latter, and not the former, is the goal of matured beings. Just as a vine that expends its whole energy on producing wood and leaves misses its purpose, so the soul that surrenders to God, that receives and develops, but stops short at giving itself away to man in a life of sacrifice, frustrates the very purpose of the union which God has made possible to such sour-grape bearers as we must ever be, apart from vital union with Him who is the Sweet Vine. True union will, by a great spiritual law, be followed by abundant fruitfulness.

Marriage to Jesus will be followed by *likeness.* Just as in true wedded life, the husband and wife become assimilated to each other in affinities, choices, mental peculiarities, and even in physiognomy, so, by being "a partaker of Christ," we become of necessity Christ-like. "When God set forth His only begotten Son as the only possible way of access to Himself, it meant that He can have delight in, or have fellowship with, nothing in which the likeness of His Son is not to be seen. We can have no further entrance into God's favor or good pleasure than He can see Christ in us." "But we all, with unveiled face mirroring the glory of the Lord, are changed into the same image from glory to glory, even as by the Lord the Spirit" (2 Cor. 3:18). The apostle's thought seems to be, not the reflection and radiation of the light and beauty of Christ, but the receiving and taking into ourselves that which is presented to our vision. Just as the mirror seems to hold the face that looks into it, so we, opening our nature to Jesus, begin to mirror Him therein, for with His likeness He comes in the person of His transfiguring Spirit to dwell and work in us, until the same likeness as that which He bears is wrought out and perfected in us; the glory and loveliness in Him become glory and loveliness in us, and from the centre to the very circumference of our being we are transfigured.

In this marriage the *wealth* of the Husband is of course placed at the disposal of the wife. Many will remember the story of the Lord of Burleigh which Tennyson has immortalized. Under the guise of a landscape painter he won the heart of a simple village maiden. Imagining they were going to the cottage of which he had spoken, in which they were to spend their happy wedded life, they pass one beautiful dwelling after another, until

>...a gateway she discerns
>With armorial bearings stately,
>    And beneath the gate she turns;
>Sees a mansion more majestic
>    Than all those she saw before:
>Many a gallant gay domestic
>    Bows before him at the door.
>And they speak in gentle murmur,
>    When they answer to his call,
>While he treads with footstep firmer,
>    Leading on from hall to hall.
>And while now she wonders blindly,
>    Nor the meaning can divine,
>Proudly turns he round and kindly,
>    "All of this is mine and thine."

So by this union of hearts and lives the simple village girl had become the Lady of Burleigh, and all her husband's wealth was hers.

Who shall tell of the wealth which they inherit who are truly united to Jesus! St. Paul speaks in his Ephesian letter of the *exceeding* riches of His grace (Eph. 2:7). Then he speaks of the *unsearchable* riches of Christ (3:8). The word translated "exceeding" literally means "to shoot beyond the mark"; St. Paul means, that though we use the utmost wealth of language, we cannot shoot beyond the mark: the riches of which he is thinking exceed all power of language to express. In the other passage, the word "*unsearchable*" literally means riches that can never be explored. We can not only not calculate them, but we can never get to the end of our investigation. When we have carried our search to the limits of possibility, there is still a vast continent of riches lying unexplored before us. And as our heavenly Bridegroom leads us on, He will be ever bringing home to us some new discovery of our wealth in Him, and at each new revealing He will say: *"All of this is Mine and thine."*

It follows that the *protection* of the husband is the marriage portion of the wife. Bride of Jesus, let no danger ever affright thee! "No weapon that is formed against thee can prosper; and every tongue that shall rise against thee in judgment thou shalt condemn" (Isa. 54:17). Jesus, thy husband, is invested with absolute authority over this world. All the forces of nature are in His hands. All the powers of what we call natural laws are under His control. All the forces of evil are under His feet. He holds the scepter in His hands, and He controls, governs, and manages, with absolute power, everything that pertains to the history of our race, and to the interests of those whom He has redeemed with His precious blood. He speaks of three gifts in His High-priestly prayer: "As Thou hast given Him power over all flesh, that He should give eternal life to as many as Thou hast given Him" (John 17:2). By the first He is invested with the government of the world; by the second, we who trust in Him for salvation are given to Him; by the third, He communicates to all such eternal life. It is in order that the last gift may be communicated that Christ is clothed with universal power.

Not I, but Christ, be honored, loved, exalted,
    Not I, but Christ, be seen, be known, be heard,
Not I, but Christ, in every look and action,
    Not I, but Christ, in every thought and word.

Not I, but Christ, to gently soothe in sorrow,
    Not I, but Christ, to wipe the falling tear,
Not I, but Christ, to lift the weary burden,
    Not I, but Christ, to hush away all fear.

Not I, but Christ, no idle word e'er falling,
    Christ, only Christ, no needless bustling sound,
Christ, only Christ, no self-important bearing,
    Christ, only Christ, no trace of I be found.

Not I, but Christ, my every need supplying,
    Not I, but Christ, my strength and health to be;
Christ, only Christ, for body, soul, and spirit,
    Christ, only Christ, live then Thy life in me.

Christ, only Christ, ere long will fill my vision;
    Glory excelling soon, full soon I'll see
Christ, only Christ, my every wish fulfilling—
    Christ, only Christ, my all in all to be.
                            —A. B. SIMPSON

CHAPTER 17

# "Not I, But Christ"

AUGUSTINE was one day after his conversion seen in the street by a woman with whom he had associated in his life of sin, and as he saw her he started to run. She ran after him, and cried: "Augustine, why do you run, it is I!" And Augustine replied: "I run because I am not I." The goal to which the Holy Spirit leads every new-born soul is that which is so strikingly expressed by St. Paul in the familiar words which are at the head of this chapter: "Not I, but Christ." The human I is not perfected by any such progress as we have sought to describe, and as some have so strangely concluded; it is delivered over to death, and by the power of the Holy Ghost is ever kept in the place of death, while Christ takes the place of the I, and reigns supremely on the throne of the being, the entire government of which is on His shoulders.

There is no more important question among the many which gather round this subject, than this: How is it possible so to live that those around us will always see "Not I, but Christ." We believe the answer is largely found in what St. Paul calls the "putting on" of Christ.

Just as among weeds, some that are painted with alluring colors are only weeds still, so among the fruits of the natural life are some that carry a more specious appearance than others, but they are nevertheless the growth of the carnal mind. Augustine spoke strongly, but none too strongly, when he said: "Our very virtues are but splendid sins." "The affections, beautiful as they are in the place they occupy in the mental structure, and important and interesting as they are in their outward office, have felt, like every other part of our mental being, the effects of our depraved and fallen condition. They sometimes fall below their appropriate strength; but more frequently err, either in being wrongly directed, or in being inordinately strong. It is evident, from a slight inspection of what human nature everywhere presents to our notice, that they require a constant regulation; in other words, they need to be sanctified."[1]

When Ignatius exclaimed: "My love is crucified!" he meant that his natural, earthly affection—with all the passions appertaining to it—hung on the Cross, and that he had claimed, and received in its stead, a heavenly and immortal love. Why is there such a lack of love among Christians? Why is the badge of true discipleship so seldom seen? Is it not because God's children have not learned to put off the old love, that is so limited in its power of expression, and so easily provoked, and to put on the love of Jesus "which is not provoked, which thinketh no evil, beareth all things, believeth all things, hopeth all things, endureth all things, which never faileth?"

"Whoso dieth to all likeness of nature," says Tauler, "his flow or efflux is Divine love, and his influx or ebb is also Divine love. It happens thus that men not dead to themselves often love by nature, weening it is by grace, and when they are blamed for this, they are troubled and wax wroth; by this they should know that their love is natural. For right Divine love is at all times patient, and suffereth all things; it letteth itself quite well be hated, but it hateth no one, and construeth all things for the best; but men not dead to themselves are always agitated in contradiction, and distracted from their peace."

The putting off of our sin-tainted and defective human love, and the appropriation of the love of God in Jesus Christ, will save us from what has been called inordinate *partialities;* in other words, those particular attachments to certain persons which generally exist without adequate reason, and which are apt to be attended with corresponding dislikes to other persons. When we do make a difference in our confidence and affection, it will be for reasons and on grounds which God can approve.

The secret of possessing an unfailing love is to claim the fulfillment, moment by moment, of Christ's own desire, "That the love wherewith Thou hast loved Me may be *in them,* and I *in them*" (John 17:26). The indwelling of Jesus, and the indwelling of Divine Love, are conceived of here as one and the same thing, and they truly are inseparable. The conditions on which this love may become ours are clearly revealed. They are *separation from the world:* "They are not of the world, even as I am not of the world" (v. 16); *obedience to the Word:* "The words which Thou gavest Me I have given unto them, and they received them" (v. 8); and *unity with the children of God:* "That they may be one" (v. 22).

What has been said about natural and Divine love applies also to human and Divine patience. How much of perturbation is introduced into a man's own life, and into the lives of all those who immediately surround him, if he knows nothing of the art of appropriating the patience of Jesus. If a meal is a few minutes late, or a cabman is unavoidably hindered either in keeping or carrying out an engagement; if a sermon is a little longer than usual, or one whose salvation is sought is unusually intractable and perverse, the human patience is very quickly strained to the breaking point. This is ever to the loss and hurt of not one but *many* individuals; for, as we have suggested, the impatient spirit never suffers alone.

Is not this manifestation of impatience the revelation of a spirit that still largely revolves round the human I? Unquestionably it is, and there is but one remedy, the persistent claiming of death to self, and the daily putting on of the lamb-like patience of Jesus Christ. Living perpetually in the center of God's will, nothing can put our patience to the test but by His ordering or permission, and when the train is late or the letter miscarries, we have opportunity to prove whether our patience is creaturely or Divine, whether it belongs to the old man or the new. "Not without design does God write the music of our lives. Be it ours to learn the time, and not be discouraged at the *rests*. If we say sadly to ourselves, 'There is no music in a rest,' let us not forget *there is the making of music in it*. The making of music is often a slow and painful process in this life. How patiently God works to teach us! How long He waits for us to learn the lesson."[2]

Human kindliness and generosity is frequently at fault. Good is often attempted from the mere impulse of nature. Sometimes far too much money, for example, is given to one object, and sometimes far too little or nothing whatever is given to one whose necessities are crying for urgent relief, for no other reason, it may be, than that our kindness has been imposed upon. Unsanctified generosity will often thus fail of its object, doing harm rather than good. We may do the right thing at the right time, if in this matter also we put on the wisdom and generosity of Jesus Christ. God holds the remedy of the evils which exist in the world in His own hands. He employs His people as instruments in applying this remedy. But the application is never made beneficially, either to the subject or the agent, except when it is made under God's own superintendence, and in His own time and manner.

This "putting on" process is frequently referred to in both the Old and New Testaments (see Isa. 59:16, 17; 61:10; Psa. 132:16; Zech. 3:1-5; Luke 15:22; Rom. 13:14; Eph. 4:22-24; Col. 3:8-14; Rev. 19:8). It is evident from a reference to these passages, that death-fellowship with Christ is equivalent to putting off the old man, and life-fellowship with Him equivalent to putting on the new man. The word "habit," which originally meant clothing, now signifies the garniture of the soul. "The conscience, the affections, the will, the thoughts, are the looms in the soul, and by their incessant activity are weaving out a subtle fabric of moral qualities which clothes the soul with conduct appropriate to itself."

We cannot put on the new *over* the old, as some have strangely taught. The old man waxeth corrupt according to the lusts of deceit, and if we do not put him off he will wrap his poisonous vesture about us—which, according to its inmost nature, will wax more and more corrupt—until we have reached that fixity of character which is described as filthiness (Rev. 22:11). The new man, on the contrary, is, by a continuous process, "being renewed unto knowledge after the image of Him that created him" (Col. 3:9, RV). And this transformation into His wondrous likeness is the end of all our putting off and putting on.

We cannot be too frequently reminded that it is only by "putting on" Christ that we "put off" self. Our moral nature abhors the vacuum that would be created by an old affection taking its departure from the innermost chambers of our being, without any new affection to succeed it. The old monarch—the imperious I—will retain his position until the new monarch—Incarnate Love—is invited to supplant the tyrant, restore tranquility, and enthrone Himself in our nature. The ruling monarch will not abdicate at a mandate from the chair of reason; nothing can displace him but the all-victorious rivalship of Jesus, whose love is the divinely appointed prescription for the exorcism of self. "He died for all, *that they which live should not henceforth live unto themselves,* but unto Him who died for them and rose again." "I saw," said George Fox, "a sea of light, and a sea of ink; and the sea of light flowed into the sea of ink, and swept it away for ever."

Love took up the Harp of Life, and played on all its
chords with might—
Touched the chord of Self, which passed in music
out of sight.

We cannot close this chapter more appropriately than by quoting
the words of that robust thinker and manly Christian, the lamented
Dr. R. W. Dale. "We must 'put away' our old self. It is not in a single
limb or a single organ that we are affected; the very springs of life are
foul; corruption has already set in. The whole structure of our former
moral character and habits must be demolished and the ruins cleared
away, that the building may be recommenced from its very foundation. We are to *put on* Christ. *We are to make our own every separate
element of His righteousness and holiness.* We are to make His humility
ours, and His courage, His gentleness, and His invincible integrity; His
abhorrence of sin, and His mercy for the penitent; His delight in the
righteousness of others, and His patience for their infirmities; the quiet
submission with which He endured His own sufferings, and His compassion for the sufferings of others; His indifference to ease and wealth
and honor, and His passion for the salvation of men from all their sins
and all their sorrows. We are to make His perfect faith in the Father
ours, and His perfect loyalty to the Father's authority; His delight in
doing the Father's will; His zeal for the Father's glory. The perfection at
which we have to aim is not a mere dream of the imagination, but the
perfection which human nature has actually reached in Christ. Christ's
human perfection was really human, but it was the translation into a
human character and history of the life of God. He is living still. The
fountains of my life are in Him. It is the eternal purpose of the Father,
that as the branch receives and reveals the life which is in the vine, I
should receive and reveal the life which is in Christ. When, therefore,
I attempt to 'put on' Christ, or to make my own the perfect humanity
which God created in Him, I am not attempting to imitate a perfection
which in spirit and form may be alien from my own moral tempera-
ment and character, and which may be altogether beyond my strength;
I am but developing a life and energy which God has already given to
me. If I am in Christ, the spiritual forces which were illustrated in the

righteousness and holiness of Christ's life are already active in my own life.

"But these forces are not mere instincts which act blindly and unintelligently; they require the control and direction of the reason, illuminated by the Spirit of God. They do not render moral effort unnecessary; they make moral effort in its most energetic form possible, and they achieve their triumph by sustaining a vigorous and unceasing endeavor after moral and spiritual perfection. *Christ is the prophecy of our righteousness* as well as the Sacrifice for our sins."[3]

> Above the chant of priests;
> Above the blatant tongues of braying doubt,
> We hear the still, small voice of love,
> Which sends its simple message out:
> And dearer, sweeter, day by day,
> Its mandate echoes from the skies:
> *'Go roll the stone of self away,*
> And let the Christ in you arise.'

In America, when people are uncertain about anything, they say "I guess," but when they know a thing to be accurate, they say "I reckon." It shows there is an element of intelligence about it. There are some of us who are very bad at reckoning; but all may reckon thus. One of the simplest things in the world is this, "Twice one are two." There is eternal truth underneath this. All the mathematicians in the world cannot make $2 + 2 = 5$. Therefore, there is eternal unchangeableness and reliable truth at the basis of this simple reckoning. I make out three things in the process. First, fix your mind upon this figure, this symbol of a number, 2. Secondly, in its relation to that other figure 2, 2 and 2. What is the third absolute certainty? Something that once seen, you never can unsee. 2 and 2 make 4. "Likewise reckon ye yourselves to be dead indeed unto sin, but alive unto God, through our Lord Jesus Christ." The reckoning has to do with my need here, and with that great full salvation there. Now, let us see. I put down this first of all. "God has *power* to cleanse my soul from all sin, and make me live to Himself." Is that a positive thing? That I might put down as number 2. Very well, God has in the redemption of the Lord Jesus Christ made an ample, adequate *provision* for the cleansing of my soul. That also is 2. The next thing is this. God has *promised* in His Word, in unequivocal English, that He will cleanse my soul from all sin, and make me thoroughly alive to Him. That is the third figure. What is the fourth? God who has this power, God who has provided this salvation, God who has given this promise is faithful, He is "God that cannot lie." Now, I come up to these figures and I say, here is my amazing need, my unutterable depth of need for cleansing and fullness of love. Here is the power of God through the redemption of Jesus Christ. Here is God's promise, and here, covering all, the absolute faithfulness of God. Twice 1 are 2, twice 2 are 4. Lord, I believe.

—Isaac E. Page

CHAPTER 18

# Reckoning at the Cross

WHEN the suspension bridge across the Niagara was to be erected, the question how to get the cable over was solved by a favoring wind. A kite was elevated, which alighted on the other shore. To its insignificant strand a cord was attached which was drawn over, then a rope, and finally a cable, strong enough to sustain the iron cable which supported the bridge, over which heavily-laden trains passed to and fro in perfect safety. Standing within sight of the Cross, and beginning to comprehend what the Sin-bearer's death means to us, we begin a reckoning, which, as Professor Beet says, "may seem at first akin to madness," but which is so wonderfully honored on God's side, that what at first was like that tiny strand, increases and strengthens by the law of habit, until it becomes an unshakable medium of intercourse between ourselves and God.

Let us notice some of the laws which govern the exercise of this vital principle which we call faith.

We are so constituted, that it is not possible for us to put forth a volition to do anything which at the same time we believe it impossible to do. Our volition will be weakened or strengthened, moreover, in proportion as our belief in the practicability or impracticability of what is proposed is strong or weak. A strong faith will make a strong will, and a weak faith a weak will. If we question for a moment the obtainability of such a life as we have been thinking about, we immediately cut the strands of that bridge across which we may communicate with God, and be the recipients of His choicest communications to us. It was because men believed in the practicability of the Niagara bridge that it was accomplished. The faith that overcame the barriers to its erection was natural; the faith we are called upon to exercise is religious, because it is directed to religious objects; and if natural faith is mighty, faith that fastens itself upon God is almighty. Religious faith takes hold of the infinite God, and every element of His nature is pledged in the behalf of the man or woman who says, "*I believe God.*" That definition of faith so frequently heard, as "taking God at His Word," *may* mean nothing more than taking the Word as God's. A key is only of value as we use it for the lock and door we want to open; and the Word is the key which introduces us to direct and living contact with God Himself. It is in this fellowship with God that we hear His voice speaking the promise, and when we have heard God speak, it is easy to believe His Word.

Unbelief has always a moral cause, and this entrance into God's presence so as to hear and believe His voice is only possible when we have put away from our lives everything, whether sinful or doubtful, that is out of harmony with His will. The three great lines of self-surrender are: to be anything the Lord wants us to *be;* to do anything He wants us to *do;* to suffer anything He wants us to *suffer.* These embrace the subjective, the active, and the passive forms of our existence, and every point in each line must be yielded, however severe the struggle may be.

The crucial point with many is the surrender of the will. This is the backbone of our being, the arbiter of the soul, the grand marshal of the faculties, and, until fully yielded to God, is strong when it ought to be weak, and weak when it ought to be strong. But our will must be surrendered, and God's will must be accepted, that "good and acceptable and perfect will of God." It has been put thus. Here is a circle which represents His will. I voluntarily place myself in the center of it, and resolve to *be* what God wills, to *do* what God wills, to *suffer* what God wills. I renounce my own plans and preferences and programs, and accept His. Whatever comes to me, comes to me through His will, so long as by an obedient walk and an unfaltering faith I maintain the position I have taken. Should an unkind letter reach me, it reaches me through His will; should the angel of death darken my home, he visits me because God wills. I am in my Father's school. He has many lessons to teach me, and they are not half as hard to learn when I recognize His loving voice, and know that in weal and woe, in prosperity and adversity, in sunshine and in storm, I am safe in the center of His will.

Under these circumstances faith becomes as easy as breathing. As chemical action immediately ensues when the proper fluids come into contact with the proper metals in the electrical jar, producing the ethereal fiery current, so the moment the soul is fully yielded to God, faith springs up, spiritual action ensues, and light and life possess the heart. The story of Catherine Booth's entrance into the blessed life will illustrate what we mean. Her biographer describes the experience thus: "When we got up from our knees I lay on the sofa exhausted with the excitement and effort of the day. William said, 'Don't you lay all on the altar?' I replied, 'I am sure I do.' Then he said, 'And isn't the altar holy?' I replied in the language of the Holy Ghost, 'The altar is most holy; whatsoever touches it is holy.' 'Then,' said he, 'are you not holy?' I replied, with my heart full of emotion and with some faith, 'Oh, I think I am.' Immediately the word was given me to confirm my faith. 'Now you are clean through the Word which I have spoken unto you.' And I took hold—true, with a trembling hand and not unmolested by the tempter—but I held fast my confidence and it grew stronger, and from that moment I have dared to reckon myself dead indeed unto sin, and alive unto God through Jesus Christ my Lord."

When thus perfectly yielded to God on every point, for time and for eternity, there is nothing to hinder this reckoning of faith and the laying of our offending nature upon the altar of Christ's Cross for entire destruction. From that moment we may begin—in the utter absence of feeling or emotion—to reckon ourselves "dead unto sin and alive unto God through Jesus Christ;" for the two key-words of the wonderful message in Romans 6 are *"yield"* and *"reckon."* Let us quote here the words of that clear teacher, Professor Upham: "As soon as men open the door by removing the strong and indurated bolt of their worldly affections, He comes quicker than His own lightnings, and claims His seat of dominion in the inner soul. It is done so quickly that there is no longer an opportunity to look for Him abroad. *There He is,* rejoicing in His recovered position; forgetting and forgiving all the injury and guilt of His exclusion; purifying and beautifying the mansion which had been stained with the world's dark sin, and rent with its stormy sorrow."

"Having therefore these promises, beloved, let us cleanse ourselves from all defilement of flesh and spirit, perfecting holiness in the fear of God" (2 Cor. 7:1). The prompt decisive act is represented by the phrase "let us cleanse," which is in the *aorist*—a tense which denotes singleness of act, a point in the expanse of time. The patient, gradual, maturing work is expressed in the phrase which follows: "carrying holiness to completion in the fear of God."

In 1765 John Wesley answered the question, "What shall we do in order that this work of God may be wrought in us?" as follows: "In this, as in all other instances, by grace are ye saved *through faith*. Full sanctification is not of works, lest any man should boast. It is the gift of God, and it is to be received by *plain, simple faith*. First, believe that God has *promised* to save you from all sin and to fill you with Himself. Until we are thoroughly satisfied of this, there is no moving one step farther. Secondly, believe that He is *able* thus to save completely all who come to Him through Christ. Admitting that with men this is impossible, this creates no difficulty in the case, seeing with God all things are possible. Thirdly, believe He is *willing* to do it now. Is not a moment to Him the same as a thousand years? He cannot want more time to accomplish whatever is His will. Fourthly, believe that He does it *now*. Not at any distant time, not when you come to die, not tomorrow, but today. He will then enable you to believe *it is done*, according to His word."

A great difficulty with many is in the maintenance of this reckoning, until the act of faith grows into a habit, and sinful habits are replaced by those that are of the Spirit of God. Let us recall the illustration on page 63. The plant has condemned a leaf to decay, and the moment the silting-up process begins, the leaf is doomed. It may be weeks before it falls off, but it is as good as dead already. The plant never goes back on its resolve, if we may so put it, to deny that leaf further nourishment, and throw its sap in another direction. Let us learn the lesson. Evil habits, which are the growth of years, are doomed the moment we put the Cross of Christ between ourselves and them, and if we keep the Cross there, *never going back on our first reckoning,* the fate of these sinful habits is irrevocably sealed, even though for weeks they may seek to regain their former ascendency.

This is a matter which concerns the *will*, and when the will trembles obediently on the verge of action, the infinite resources of God are at its disposal in an instant. When the paralytic *willed* to stretch forth his withered hand, God's enabling power came in between the act of willing and the act of stretching forth. Reckon on God, and throw the responsibility on Him.

A gentleman was riding with his host. The host wanted to return home by a certain road, but there was a difficulty. The chestnut mare his guest was riding refused to pass a certain bridge. She had been tried again and again, but always in vain. The host suddenly remembered that his guest was what he called "a praying man," and he thought he had an opportunity of testing the power of prayer. Was it worth anything in an exigency of this sort? The man of God was quite willing to trust his Lord, and away they rode. Hastening across the bridge, the host turned to see a struggle and perchance a victory over a nervous horse. But there was victory without struggle. He saw his friend *drop the reins* on the mare's neck as they came to the bridge, and heard him say, as he looked upwards, "Now, Lord!" and quietly as a lamb the mare crossed the bridge. Let us reckon thus on God, and when the bridge has to be crossed, let us learn to drop the reins, and casting the responsibility on Him, say, "Now, Lord!" and He *cannot* fail because He *cannot* deny Himself.

Are children trained
Only that they may reach some higher class?
Only for some few schoolroom years that pass
 Till growth is gained?
Is it not rather for the years beyond
To which the father looks with hopes so fair and fond?

 He traineth so
That we may shine for Him in this dark world,
And bear His standard dauntlessly unfurled:
 That we may show
His praise, by lives that mirror back His love,
His witnesses on earth, as He is ours above.

 Not only here
The rich result of all our God doth teach
His scholars, slow at best, until we reach
 A nobler sphere:
Then, not till then, our training is complete,
And the true life begins for which He made us meet.

 Look on to this
Through all perplexities of grief and strife,
To this, thy true maturity of life,
 Thy coming bliss;
That such high gifts thy future dower may be,
And for such service high thy God prepareth thee.

—F. R. HAVERGAL

CHAPTER 19

# The School of Obedience

IT is a noteworthy fact that whenever the example of Christ is presented to us in Scripture for our imitation, it is His example in suffering. "Let this mind be in you," says St. Paul, "which was also in Christ Jesus." All the features of the disposition which He thus sets before us for imitation have to do with self-renunciation. We see suffering carved on every step Jesus took, until he reached the lowest, and "became obedient unto death, even the death of the Cross" (Phil. 2:5-8). To suffer patiently for well-doing is, St. Peter says, "acceptable with God. For even hereunto were ye called; because Christ also suffered for us, leaving us an example, that ye should follow His steps" (1 Peter 2:20, 21). "Forasmuch then," says the same writer, "as Christ hath suffered for us in the flesh, arm yourselves likewise with the same mind" (1 Peter 4:1). "Beloved, think it not strange," he says yet again, "concerning the fiery trial which is to try you, as though some strange thing happened unto you: but rejoice, inasmuch as ye are partakers of Christ's sufferings" (1 Peter 4:12, 13).

The reason for this noteworthy fact is given in Hebrews 5:8, 9: "Though He were a Son, yet learned He obedience by the things which He suffered; and being made perfect, He became the Author of eternal salvation unto all them that obey Him." In other words, we can only become possessed of the mind of Jesus by going into the same school, by putting ourselves into the hands of the same teachers, and by joyfully submitting ourselves to the same discipline.

There is great danger lest the preciousness and indispensableness of the experience of suffering should be not sufficiently emphasized. It is pleasant and easy to learn obedience under some teachers, but before we have graduated in this school we must pass into the hands of others whose lessons are not pleasant or easy; we must go out of the sunshine into the darkened room; gladness and joy must give place to anguish and soul-travail, and through an experience of suffering from which, perchance, we start and shrink we learn obedience.

What does this learning of obedience mean? The principle of obedience is one thing, and the application of it is another. The disposition of obedience Jesus possessed before He suffered, but the proof that the disposition existed must be shown in deed, and the progress from the disposition to the deed was the practical learning of the virtue of obedience.

The first question is, how may the zone of obedience be reached so that not on nine occasions out of ten we shall say "yes" to God, but that we shall never say aught but "yes" to Him? The answer to this question has been given in earlier chapters, and it will suffice here if we say simply that the usurping monarch Self must be completely vanquished and deposed, by inviting and trusting Jesus to take the throne of the heart. It is only when He has come to purify, to possess, and to rule, that we are able to say: "All that the Lord hath said will we do, and be obedient."

As Isaac Pennington says: "The holy skill of obeying the truth is hid from all living but such as are begotten and brought up in the mystery of subjection to the Lord. 'Thy people shall be willing in the day of Thy power.' It is the power of God that works the *will* in the heart, and the same power works to *do* also (Phil. 2:13); and none can learn either to will or to do aright, but as they come to be acquainted with that power, joined to that power, and feel that power working in them. *In this power holy obedience is as natural as disobedience is to the birth of the flesh.* Blessed be the name of the Lord."

Obedience, to be perfect, must be submitted to test. You cannot call a child obedient if his obedience has never cost him anything; nor do you know that he will obey when the trial comes unless he has been already put to the test, and so has had an opportunity of applying the principle which existed in his heart. In this progress from the principle to the application, from the disposition to the deed, there is, and must be, suffering.

The Divine nature of Jesus could not be perfected—that was perfect already; but human nature is born weak and undeveloped, and it has to grow. One of its essential laws is its capability of improvement, and thus it was that Jesus, by passing through a long curriculum of trial and suffering, learned obedience. He could only learn obedience by becoming incarnate, by stooping to share our discipline, and bearing the Divine will as a yoke, instead of wielding it as a scepter. His obedience was perfected by suffering, and with His obedience His human character. The means produced the end with Him that it might produce the self-same end with us, and from the moment of His perfection Jesus consecrated suffering as a minister of the Divine purpose, so that His followers need no longer shrink from and tremble at it, but rather glory in and welcome it as a conquered foe that has become their friend.

There are different ways, as a great teacher reminds us, both of knowing and of learning. "A large part of our knowledge is either intuitive and ideal, residing in the pure reason; or speculative—that is, gathered by deduction and mental inference. Another kind is learned by what we call life—by experience, personal trial, entanglement with events, struggles in doing and suffering; and what we learn in this way we know with a depth and familiarity far beyond all other knowledge: it is now part of our living energies and powers, and dwells in our very being. Not only is its stamp imprinted on us, but it so passes into us as to blend with our whole inner nature. *We are* what we have done and suffered."

To shrink, therefore, from suffering is to shrink from what is a requisite part of our education both for earth and for heaven. We shall be spiritual babes all our lives, spelling out nothing but the alphabet of Divine truth, if we refuse to drink of the cup of which Jesus drank, and to be baptized with the baptism that He was baptized with, for "it became Him for whom are all things, and by whom are all things, in bringing many sons unto glory, to make the Captain of their salvation perfect through sufferings." He could not have become our Leader and Captain had He not trod the rough road He calls upon us to tread. Exemption from suffering would have meant exemption from Leadership. He could not have lifted us into a share of His glory had He not stooped to the companionship of our griefs; nor can we rightly call ourselves His soldiers unless we are following in His steps, or expect to be lifted into the companionship of His glory unless we are among those who know the "fellowship of His sufferings."

We have spoken of suffering as the school of obedience, and of this experience as absolutely necessary to the completion of our education both for the earthly and heavenly service. It is necessary for service on earth. It is because Jesus "suffered being tempted" that He is "able to succor them that are tempted." "If ever I fall into a surgeon's hands with broken bones," is a remark which has become almost proverbial, "give me one whose own bones have been broken." To take our degree in the school of obedience means a qualifying for such a ministry as would be otherwise impossible; and what work is more to be coveted or necessary than that of feeling with, comforting, and sustaining those whom God counts worthy of the honor of suffering.

Of our ministry in the other life we know but little, for "it doth not yet appear what we shall be." This we do know, however: the lessons we have learned here will not be lost there, and in the service of heaven we shall be eternally thankful for the schooling of earth. Nothing will give us greater comfort than to remember this. *We* have a clearly defined purpose in expending time, money, and skill upon *our* children in their earlier years. And no lesson is without its value, either in the disciplining of the mind, the acquisition of knowledge, or the formation of character. We may be certain that God has a clearly defined plan, both for the present and future life, for everyone of His children; that no lesson, however seemingly trivial or important, pleasant or painful, is purposeless; and that "*all things* are for our advantage."

Sometime, when all life's lessons have been learned,
    And sun and stars for evermore have set,
The things which our weak judgments here have spurned,
    The things o'er which we grieved with lashes wet,
Will flash before us out of life's dark night,
    As stars shine most in deeper tints of blue,
And we shall see how all God's plans are right,
    And how what seemed reproof was love most true.

And you shall shortly know that lengthened breath
Is not the sweetest gift God sends His friend;
And that, sometimes, the sable pall of death
    Conceals the fairest boon His love can send.
If we could push ajar the gates of life,
    And stand within, and all God's workings see,
We could interpret all this doubt and strife,
    And for each mystery could find a key.

But not today. Then be content, poor heart!
    God's plans, like lilies pure and white, unfold;
We must not tear the close-shut leaves apart,
    Time will reveal the calyxes of gold;
And if, through patient toil, we reach the land
    Where tired feet, with sandals loosed, may rest,
Where we shall clearly see and understand—
    I think that we shall say, "God knew the best."
            —MAY RILEY SMITH

CHAPTER 20

# The Tests of Obedience

GOD always has a number of His children under examination. Some of them pass with honors, but not a few are turned back to learn their lessons over again. Many fail in this critical time in their spiritual history through failure to understand the Divine purpose. They cry out with Job: "He hath fenced up my way that I cannot pass, He hath set darkness in my paths." They do not perceive that the position they have taken over and over again is being put to the test.

Madame Guyon puts it thus: "God will give us opportunities to try our consecration, whether it be a true one or not. No man can be wholly the Lord's unless he is wholly consecrated to the Lord; and no man can know whether he is thus wholly consecrated except by *tribulation*. That is the test. To rejoice in God's will, when that will imparts nothing but happiness, is easy even for the natural man. But none but the renovated man, none but the religious man, can rejoice in the Divine will when it crosses his path, disappoints his expectations, and overwhelms him with sorrow. Trial therefore, instead of being shunned, should be welcomed as the test—and the only true test—of a true state. Beloved souls, there are consolations which pass away, but true and abiding consolation ye will not find except in entire abandonment, and in that love which loves the Cross. He who does not welcome the Cross does not welcome God."

How many have repeatedly and deliberately said to God: "I put myself wholly into Thy hands: put me to what Thou wilt; rank me with whom Thou wilt; put me to doing, put me to suffering; let me be employed for Thee, or laid aside for Thee; exalted for Thee, or trodden under foot for Thee; let me be full, let me be empty; let me have all things, let me have nothing; I freely and heartily resign *all* to Thy pleasure and disposal."

In due time God takes us at our word. He has had us in His school for months, or it may be for years, and has given us great freedom and joy. He has set our feet in a "large place" of blessing, when suddenly, perhaps, suffering of the severest character takes the place of the delightful experiences through which we have been passing. The vessel which has been sailing under fair and sunny skies is struck by a hurricane, and her staunchness is tested to the uttermost.

Among the many comforting words in such a season, that of the apostle James is most sustaining. He says: "Count it all joy, my brethren, when ye fall into manifold trials; knowing that the proof of your faith worketh patience. And let patience have its perfect work, that ye may be perfect and entire, lacking in nothing" (James 1:2-4). Note the condition, surrounded by *"manifold trials."* Out of surroundings which have been conducive to peace, comfort, and outward prosperity, we suddenly fall into the midst of a marauding band of trials. We seem, as one says, to be "left to the heartlessness of a thousand petty demons, who pervade every little circumstance; who seem, like the fabled Liliputians, to tie our hands and feet while we sleep; who snap all the threads of our financial looms; who upset our ordinary plans; who turn anticipated joys into ashes. There are times when a current of such things seems to set in; times when everything seems to weave itself into a network of crippling environment, and any effort to extricate ourselves only bruises us."

We are tempted to be terrified by our adversaries, to despise the chastening of the Lord, to grow weary of His correction, and to faint in the day of adversity. To prevent our yielding to either of these temptations, God has clearly revealed His purpose, and has distinctly told us what our attitude should be. If ever we needed to listen for the voice of Infinite Love it is now. Listen, He speaks: "Fear not: for I have redeemed thee, I have called thee by thy name; thou art Mine. When thou passest through the waters, I will be with thee; and through the rivers, they shall not overflow thee: when thou walkest through the fire, thou shalt not be burned; neither shall the flame kindle upon thee. For I am the Lord thy God, the Holy One of Israel, thy Saviour" (Isa. 43:1-3).

In giving a lecture on Flame, a scientist once made a most interesting experiment. He wanted to show that in the center of each flame is a hollow, a place of entire stillness, around which its fire is a mere wall. To prove this he introduced into the midst of the flame a minute and carefully shielded charge of explosive powder. The protection was then carefully removed, and no explosion followed. The charge was again shielded and withdrawn. A second time the experiment was tried, and by a slight agitation of the hand the central security was lost, and an immediate explosion told the result. Our safety, then, is only in the stillness of soul. If we are affrighted and exchange the principle of faith for that of fear, or if we are rebellious and restless we shall be hurt by the flames, and anguish and disappointment will be the result.

Moreover, God will be disappointed in us if we break down. Testing is a proof of His love and confidence, and who can tell what pleasure our steadfastness and stillness give to Him? If He allowed us to go without testing it would be no compliment to our spiritual experience. Much trial and suffering means, therefore, that God has confidence in us; that He believes we are strong enough to endure; that we shall be true to Him even when He has left us without any outward evidence of His care, and at the seeming mercy of our adversaries. If He increase the trials instead of diminishing them, it is an expression of confidence in us up to the present, and a further proof that He is looking to us to glorify Him in the yet hotter fires through which He is calling us to pass. Let us not be afraid. The subtleties of the self life will be exposed and the hateful thing destroyed. We shall be delivered from the outward and the transitory, and drawn into far closer fellowship with God Himself.

Think when you use the sharp blade of your penknife that its keenness has only been produced by a terribly severe process. The best steel is subjected to the alternates of extreme heat and extreme cold. That little blade was heated and hammered, then heated again, and then plunged into the coldest water to give it its right shape and temper. It would not be in your hand had it broken down under this tempering process. If, when it was put upon the grindstone, any flaw had appeared, even though previously it had seemed a perfect blade, it would have been rejected as useless, and thrown aside. So God, longing for our equipment for the *highest* service, tests us in a thousand ways. *All* things—there is no exception whatever—are working together for the purification, the refining, the testing, and the approval of human character. Now we are cast into the furnace of affliction, heated seven times hotter than it is wont to be heated; now we are plunged into the cold waters of bereavement; and now we are ground between the upper and nether stones of adversity and disaster. How shall we come forth? That depends entirely on the way we endure. If we simply say, "As God will, and in the hottest fire stand still," He will give us a place of honor among His servants, and crown us with immortal glory.

"He knoweth the way that I take, and when he hath tried me I shall come forth as gold." The hay and the stubble fear the fire, but the gold challenges the flame to do its worst. Therefore

> Let thy gold be cast in the furnace,
>    Thy red gold, precious and bright;
> Do not fear the angry fire
>    With its caverns of burning light.
> And thy gold shall return more precious,
>    Free from every spot and stain;
> For gold must be tried by the fire,
>    And the heart must be tried by pain.

The apostle James tells us what the purpose of the testing is, "That we may be perfect and entire, lacking in nothing" (1:4). "A perfect machine," says an able expositor, "fulfils the object for which it is made, and a perfect Christian is one of such a character that he fulfils the object for which he has been made a Christian. 'Entire, lacking in nothing,' conveys the idea of being properly adjusted and arranged, so that our avenues of temptation are properly guarded. A builder never thinks of putting a window in the floor, or a door in the ceiling, and God would have our moral nature so adjusted that we may have everything in its place, and consequently, 'entire, lacking in nothing.'"

Shall we shrink from an experience, however painful, which accomplishes an end like this? That which makes us mature in Christ Jesus, lacking in nothing that a Christian man should possess and enjoy, is worth any suffering, however severe or protracted. Though, therefore, we have "for a little while been put to grief in manifold trials, that the proof of our faith, being more precious than gold that perisheth, though it is proved by fire," let us, as James exhorts us, *"count it nothing but joy."* God desires not our comprehension in such times, but our confidence. He is disciplining us for eternal companionship with Himself, and because "it doth not yet appear what we shall be," let us joyfully stand in the midst of the fiery furnace, knowing that we shall lose nothing in the fire but our bonds, and that ever in the midst thereof will be One who really is the Son of God.

We shall cease to wonder at the pains God takes to purify and perfect human character, when we remember that it is the only work of His hands which, so far as we are concerned, will last for ever. Everything else that we possess and pursue is fading and perishing already. Moral character, built up under the guidance and inspiration of the Holy Spirit, partakes of God's immortality, because it is nothing less than the Divine nature incarnate, incorporated and made manifest in man.

So precious is its acquisition to God that He spares no cost to produce it. He puts us just where His purpose can best be accomplished. We sometimes complain as to the nature of our environment, but when God put us where we are He had the choice of the whole world open to Him, and could His purpose have been better achieved in other surroundings, He would have placed us there. Let us work out our salvation in thankful co-operation with Him. The diamond can offer no resistance to the cutter, nor can the clay offer intelligent response to the potter.

*We* can both resist and respond. Thankfully recognizing what Butler calls "the providential disposition of things," let us cease from the former and, with our whole heart, give ourselves to the latter.

In every congregation, in every church, throughout all Christendom, there are two classes, those who are *filled* with the Spirit of God, and those who have the Spirit but are *not filled*. What you need to do is to bow your head and let God search you with His searchlight, so that you shall get His answer to the question, "Am I filled with the Spirit?"

There is an old Romish legend of a witch who came to a new king bearing three volumes of laws, and declaring that any country governed by these laws would certainly prosper. She offered to sell these books to the king to aid him in making good laws for the Roman people; but she asked such an enormous price for them that the king refused to buy. After some time the same woman returned to the king, having burned one of the volumes, and offered to sell to him the two remaining ones. Instead, however, of asking a less sum for the two books, she greatly increased her price. Again considering it too much to pay for the coveted books, the king allowed her to go away. Once more she returned to him, this time having only one volume left. This she wanted the king to buy, but the price she asked was still further increased; indeed, it was more than she had asked for the three at the beginning. The king hesitated; but, fearing lest she should burn this last volume, he bought it up.

And so, if you refuse this blessing offered to you, it will become more and more difficult for you to obtain it. Your delay will only make the price you have to pay for it much higher in the end. Oh, if your desire to have this blessing is feeble, ask God to strengthen it, and then say, "I will have it."

—ANDREW MURRAY

# CHAPTER 21

# Filled With the Spirit

A PHILOSOPHICAL but deeply spiritual writer has pointed out that the expressions so frequently employed to indicate the experience known as that of being "filled with the Spirit" are apt to convey an erroneous impression, and that we can scarcely apply them to the mind without thinking of something which has a material shape, and, therefore, susceptible of being "filled" in the material import of the term. The operations of the Holy Spirit consequently assume a character of earthliness, becoming tangible and sensible. As those operations are spiritual in the highest sense, such views must be misleading.

Out of this misconception arises those frequently heard appeals to God for the impartation of a force which is vaguely described as "power," and which may be coveted for similar reasons to those which led Simon to offer money to the apostles for its possession. The gifts of the Spirit are far more eagerly desired by many than the graces of the Spirit, and it is quite possible to have a large supply of the former with a very small measure of the latter. No more striking Scriptural illustration of this truth can be desired than that which is found in the letters to the Corinthians.

The twelfth chapter of the first letter tells of the spiritual gifts they possessed, but chapter 13 goes on to say that unless those gifts were exercised in the spirit of love, or, in other words, in the grace of the Holy Spirit, they were nothing to God, and gave Him no joy or satisfaction. The hungry might be fed, the poor might have their wants supplied, the intellects of men might be pleased, but God's heart found no satisfaction if love was wanting. A greatly gifted man may be anything but a spiritually-minded man, and a spiritually-minded man may be far removed from "a workman that needeth not to be ashamed." The one has many gifts but little grace, the other much grace but few gifts. May we not covet from the great Giver as much of both gifts and graces as will make us usable to the Master? The full possession of the nature by the Spirit is evidenced by a purified judgment, by a loving, meek, and lowly spirit, by sanctified dispositions, in one word, by possessing the image and mind of Jesus.

Nothing has wrought more disastrously in recent years than the tendency to underestimate and even ignore the importance of the *graces* of the Spirit. Misunderstandings between Christian workers, friction and contention at home and abroad, and a woeful want of forbearance and gentleness have been the result. Nor have the disastrous effects ended here. The work of God has been hindered; the enemies of the Cross have rejoiced; and the banner of holiness, instead of flying to the breeze, has been trailing in the dust.

The fullness of the Spirit has been deemed an essential requisite for public service, but it has not been considered an essential for those home relationships where the patience, sweetness, and gentleness of Jesus are more needed than anywhere else. Who needs the unselfish spirit of Jesus more than the merchant who is surrounded by those who are always trying to take advantage of other people, and who care nothing of the disaster that comes to others if they can only enrich themselves? Shall we then seek to be filled with the Spirit, not that we may become a battery of spiritual power able to fasten truth upon a multitude of souls, but that we may love and bear, serve and suffer, where God appoints us, remembering that *to do His will* is something infinitely higher than to win hundreds of souls.

In the rooms of the American Tract Society in New York are two objects of great interest. One is a slight framework of tough wood, a few feet high, so bound together with hasps and hinges as to be taken down and folded in the hand. This was Whitefield's traveling pulpit; the one he used when, denied access to the churches, he harangued the thousands in the open air on the moors of England. You will think of this modern apostle, lifted up upon the small platform, with the throngs of eager people around him; or hurrying from one field to another, carrying his Bible in his hand; ever on the move, toiling with herculean energy, and a force like that of a giant. There, in that rude pulpit, is the symbol of all which is active and fiery in dauntless Christian zeal. The other object, resting upon the slender platform where the living preacher used to stand, is a chair—a plain, straight-backed, armed cottage-chair; rough, simple, meagerly cushioned, unvarnished, and stiff. It was the seat in which Elizabeth Wallbridge, "the Dairyman's Daughter," sat and coughed and whispered, and from which she went only at her last hour to the couch on which she died. Here again is a pulpit; and it is the symbol of a life, quiet and unromantic, and hard in all Christian endurance. Every word that invalid woman uttered—every patient night she suffered—was a Gospel sermon. *In a hundred languages the life of that servant of God has preached to millions of souls the riches of Christ's glory and grace.* And of these two pulpits, which is the most honorable is known only to God, who, undoubtedly, accepted and consecrated them both.

It is a law of dynamics that two objects cannot occupy the same space at the same time, and if we are ignorant of the crucifixion of the self-life as an experimental experience, we cannot be filled with the Holy Spirit. "If thy heart," says Arndt in his *True Christianity*, "be full of the world, there will be no room for the Spirit of God to enter; for where the one is the other cannot be." If, on the contrary, we have endorsed our Saviour's work as the destroyer of the works of the devil, and have claimed to the full the benefits of His death and risen life, what hinders the complete and abiding possession of our being by the Holy Spirit but our unbelief?

Every desire which is not of God stands like a barrier against the entrance of the Holy One to take the supreme control of our being. Let this fact be clearly recognized. All unsanctified desire constitutes a state of resistance to the Holy Spirit. When, however, the life of nature has been sanctified, Satan's dominion is effectually overthrown, and the way is open for the Spirit's triumphal entrance. His presence is now an invariable result, and He would never wait for a single hour to fill the temple of our body with His glory, were it not for the opposition which unsanctified nature presents. He stands at the door and knocks, and when His foes and ours are cast out He can say, in a sense fuller than ever before, "Lift up your heads, O ye gates, and the King of glory shall come in!" And let it be remembered it is the Holy Spirit who prepares His own habitation. He strikes the first and the last blow in this contest for the possession of redeemed men. It is He who transforms Babylon, which means *confusion,* into Salem, which means *peace;* and entering into the purified and tranquil habitation of our being, He says: "This is My rest for ever: here will I dwell, for I have desired it."

In profound thankfulness let us rejoice at His entrance, and habituate ourselves, in holy self-recollectedness, to a constant recognition of His presence. What can dishonor Him more than to doubt His incoming, and to question His abiding when all these conditions have been met?

He comes not to be our Servant but our Master; not to be at our disposal, but expecting us to be ever at His. He comes not to make us reservoirs of living water, but *aqueducts* merely. We are not like a stored-up battery of electricity, but like the telegraph wire along which the lightning can flash at any time. "God has not given me a chest of poetic gold," said Frances Ridley Havergal to one who thought she could write poetry "to order." "He keeps the gold, and gives it me piece by piece just when He will, and as much as He will and no more." "I am like a little child," she continued, "who, when writing a letter, looks up and says, 'What shall I write next?'" So we are brought to a moment by moment dependence on God, reckoning self effaced, before every act of worship or of work, and reminded of the truth, "I can do nothing out of myself." We thus become, as Rutherford puts it, "drowned debtors to His grace," or as we should perhaps put it, "over head and ears in debt to Him."

The fruit of the Spirit will of course appear under these conditions, because fruit is of the nature of the tree that produces it, and the indwelling spirit produces that in the life which is like Himself. The works of the flesh are numerous, the fruit of the Spirit is *one*.

"We may get at the Apostle's meaning concerning this indivisible fruit of the Spirit if we indulge in a little imagery. These nine features mentioned are the qualities of the fruit. Here we have the fruit before us—Love, which is the core, the very heart of the fruit; Joy is the juice; Peace is the pulp or flesh of the fruit; Long-suffering is the stalk by which it hangs; Gentleness is the scent; Goodness or Beneficence is the taste; and Faith, or rather Faithfulness or Trustworthiness, is the shape of the fruit; Meekness is the skin; Temperance—which means the completely balanced moral nature—may be the color of this fruit. The fruit of the Spirit is a beautiful growth combining all these qualities; we do not find them separate. If there is no joy, the juice is gone, and the fruit is dried and wizened; if no love, the core is gone, and the fruit is destined to be worm-eaten before long. So with each, we cannot separate them. This means that when we receive the Spirit into our hearts, we receive the germ of this fruit. The Spirit is the root or principle on which the fruit grows, and it grows without any effort of ours to produce it. It becomes our own simply by receiving it by faith."[1]

The conditions of being "filled with the Spirit" are then: First, an unshaken conviction that this is our inalienable birthright, and a determination no longer to despise it. Secondly, being restless, strengthless, and comfortless until the Spirit comes to His temple, we must begin to pant for the fullness of God as the hart pants for the water-brooks. Thirdly, here as elsewhere, death is the gate of life. Of the holy anointing oil it is written: "On man's *flesh* shall it not be poured." The Holy Spirit will not fill an unholy nature. The flesh is His immutable antagonist, and if He comes to dwell with us, He comes not to make terms with His enemy, but to destroy him utterly. Fourthly, the Holy Spirit unites Himself with the purified faculties and sanctified energies of our nature, and uses them for His glory *in proportion to our faith and faithfulness.*

"Keep step with Jesus!" Can that be for me?
Oh, may I really walk by faith with Thee?
I who have often wandered far away,
And grieved Thee with my coldness day by day?

How often, Master, I have "lagged behind,"
And feared to follow, when Thy voice so kind
Has called me on, bidding me trust in Thee,
However dark the pathway seemed to me.

And have I not sometimes stepped out *alone*,
Nor waited for Thy hand to lead me on,
And of the future thought with anxious care,
Instead of taking "the *next* step" in prayer.

Afresh today I put my hand in Thine,
With childlike trust would all to Thee resign;
Just lead me where Thou wilt and guide me still,
Fulfilling in me all Thy blessed will.
                              —E. MAY GRIMES

# CHAPTER 22

# Step by Step

PRINCIPAL Moule, in his valuable work, *Veni Creator,* reminds us that there is a speciality of phrase in the Greek word rendered "walk" in Galatians 5:25. He translates the verse, "If we live by the Spirit, let us also *take step by step by the Spirit."* Conybeare's translation is equally suggestive: "If we live by the Spirit, let our steps be guided by the Spirit." It is one thing to "live by the Spirit," to know that we have life by His power; it is another thing, in the minutest details of daily life, to yield to the authority and guidance of our Life-giver. Andrew Murray thinks these words suggest to us very clearly the difference between the sickly and the healthy Christian life. "In the former the Christian is content to 'live by the Spirit'; he is satisfied with knowing that he has the new life; but he does not walk by the Spirit. The true believer, on the contrary, is not content without having his whole walk and conversation in the power of the Spirit."

Why is the position so often taken, in those large gatherings of Christian people, now so common, not more generally maintained? How many, in a supreme moment, under the mighty power of God, throw open every avenue of their being to the incoming of the Holy Spirit! And we dare not doubt that He floods the entire being with His energy when it is thus surrendered to Him. But the experience is too often transitory, as set forth in the following lines :

> . . .There have been moments pure,
> When I have seen Thy face and felt Thy power;
> Then evil lost its grasp, and passion hushed
> Owned the Divine enchantment of the hour.
> *These were but seasons beautiful and rare."*

Why "seasons beautiful and *rare"?* Because those who thus surrender themselves, do not go away to "take step by step by the Spirit." In an unguarded moment self has been allowed to regain the supremacy, and some portions of the life have been given over to its control. Steps have been taken, not by the Spirit, but by the flesh. For a little moment, perhaps only in what seemed a trifling detail, the reins, which were unconditionally placed in the hands of the Spirit of God, were snatched out of His grasp. A grieved Spirit, and a life and work from which the power has departed, are the result.

In many cases this is more the result of carelessness than anything else. Hence the need of clearer teaching on this subject. The Christian worker has said, like Samson, "I will go out as at other times and shake myself. But he wist not that the Lord was departed from him." He finds, to his sorrow, that some subtle evil has shorn him of his strength, that some little rift within the lute has made the music mute, but how or why he scarcely knows.

John Wesley, knowing how much higher an experience it was to take step by step by the Spirit, than simply to live by the Spirit, refused to recognize the Christian perfectness of some of his converts, because they were wanting, he said, in the evidence. "They do not steadily use that kind and degree of food which they know, or might know, would most conduce to the health, strength, and vigor of the body; or they are not temperate in sleep; they do not rigorously adhere to what is best for body and mind; otherwise they would constantly go to bed and rise early, and at a fixed hour; or they sup late, which is neither good for body or soul; or they use neither fasting nor abstinence; or they prefer (which are so many forms of intemperance) that preaching, reading, or conversation which gives them transient joy and comfort, before that which brings godly sorrow or instruction in righteousness."

Many Christians have yet to learn the meaning of that word, "Whether therefore ye eat or drink, or whatsoever ye do, do *all* to the glory of God," for to take step by step by the Spirit means that our meat and drink, and everything that touches the domain of our senses, must ever be placed under a sacred discipline. This same discipline is equally indispensable for the life of our affections and thoughts; for our reading, for our recreation, for our literary and artistic pursuits. To ignore the guidance of the Holy Spirit in any of these departments of life is to cause Him grief, and to forfeit the spiritual power of which He would have us to be the unfailing aqueducts to a dying world.

Lest anyone should imagine that a life which is thus lived step by step by the Holy Spirit is an irksome one, let us say that unfailing obedience always produces unfailing joy and peace. A joyless Christian is almost invariably a disobedient Christian. "A life of self-renouncing love is a life of liberty," for where the Spirit of the Lord is—where He is recognized and obeyed in the minutiae of life—"there is liberty."

"Step by step" is the secret of a life which is never perturbed, never surprised by sudden assaults of the evil one, never shorn of its spiritual strength. With returning consciousness there is, in such a life, a resolute determination to take no step in the untrodden pathway of the day but by the Spirit. His guidance is sought and His will consulted in the choice of food. Anything that has been known to dull the spiritual vision, and unfit the body for the sacred uses for which it is designed, will be avoided. "What effect will this book have upon my spiritual life? Will it increase or diminish my relish for the Word of God?" are questions we shall ask when opportunities for reading are afforded us. "I never spend a penny," said a poor widow one day to the writer, "without asking that I may be guided how to spend it." She was seeking to take step by step by the Spirit. We need not particularize further. Here is the principle by which our life is to be governed, and to follow it will fill our life with such joy and power as we never dreamt of before.

The two realms, which men have designated secular and sacred, will "melt into each other as the roseate streaks of dawn melt into the splendors of the morning" as we take step by step by the Spirit; for when the Spirit of Christ breathes through our life, the meanest occupation becomes Divine. Nothing is little or great with regard to the things of God. Everything that bears the impress of His will is great, however trifling it may appear. It is this alone which gives value to the duties of our life, and nothing can be regarded as small or insignificant that is the object of His desire. A natural tendency to untidiness is easily overcome if, for His sake, and that we may please Him in everything, we keep the room or the papers in order.

And it is this carefulness to please God, even in the smallest trifles, that proves the reality and delicacy of our love. "We do not love perfectly when we neglect small occasions of pleasing the one whom we love, and when we do not fear to wound him by trifles. The jealousy of God is infinite; it extends to everything, and every soul that truly loves will try never to give this Divine jealousy any cause of offence."

Our life is made up of these little steps. We fancy we could be heroic on some great occasion. We could die for Christ we think, if called upon to lay down our life for Him. It is questionable, however, if we could, unless we have cultivated the martyr spirit hour by hour, for if our strength and desire to please God has failed in the trifles of our life, how can we be sure of them in the great testing-time? It is far harder to live for Christ moment by moment than it is to die once for Him; and if we wait for great occasions in which to display our fidelity, we shall find that our life has slipped away, and with it the opportunities which each hour has brought of proving our love to our Lord, by being faithful in that which is least.

It is a startling fact that if the earth were dependent upon the sun alone for heat it would not keep existence in animal and vegetable life upon its surface. The stars furnish heat enough in the course of the year to melt a crust of ice seventy feet thick—almost as much as is supplied by the sun. This seems strange when we consider how immeasurably small must be the amount of heat received from any of these distant bodies. But the surprise vanishes when we remember that the whole firmament is so thickly strewn with stars, that in some places thousands are crowded together within a space no greater than that occupied by the full moon. This illustrates the truth we have been seeking to enforce. It is to the thousands of little acts, which have been made bright because the Spirit of Christ has come into them all, that the true child of God owes the light and heat and beauty of His life.

We cannot do better than close with the following striking words of Pastor Stockmayer: "When sin or our selfness, at any distance whatever, shows itself in our horizon, when we notice something in the wind so that our moral sky, our spiritual atmosphere, is not altogether clear, let us know that it is His grace which signals the danger, His Spirit who awakens our attention. Let us stop at once; let us hasten to our refuge under the shadow of His wings; let us renewedly tighten the bonds that unite us to Him, until the light of His countenance has driven away the last vestige of the cloud, and the atmosphere has again become luminous. Be not discouraged, if at the first attempt thou failest to realize this life. Though thy communion with God be a hundred times, yea, a thousand times interrupted, do not suffer thyself to be paralyzed by these sad experiences. It is true that the wrong done to thy soul by even one momentary separation from God, such as one sin can occasion, a sin by thought, or word, or deed, is far more disastrous than thou canst know. Nevertheless there may be something worse, something which adds evil to evil, namely, permitting thyself to be discouraged instead of returning immediately to God, in order to find in Him pardon and renewing of life." "If we live by the Spirit, let us also take step by step by the Spirit."

Here is one inexhaustible paradox of this great matter; on one side a true and total self-denial, on the other, a daily need of self-crucifixion. This is a thing which I am content simply to state, and to leave it as the Lord's word upon the believer's mind and soul.

But *"daily";* without intermission, without holiday; now, today, this hour; and then, tomorrow! And the daily *"cross";* a something which is to be the instrument of disgrace and execution to something else! And what will that something be? Just whatever gives occasion of ever deeper test to the self-surrender of which we have spoken; just whatever exposes to shame and death the old aims, and purposes, and plans, the old spirit of self and its life.

Perhaps it is some small trifle of daily routine; a crossing of personal preference in very little things; accumulation of duties, unexpected interruption, unwelcome distraction. Yesterday these things merely fretted you and, internally at least, *"upset"* you. Today, on the contrary, you *take them up,* and stretch your hands out upon them, and let them be the occasion of new disgrace and deeper death for that old self-spirit. You take them up in loving, worshipping acceptance. You carry them to their Calvary in thankful submission. And tomorrow you will do the same.

—Principal Moule

# CHAPTER 23

# The Cross Day By Day

"IF any man will come after Me, let him deny himself, and take up his cross daily and follow Me" (Luke 9:23). We have spoken in the earlier chapters of this book of a Cross to which, in glad co-operation with the Holy Spirit, we nail the flesh with its passions and lusts. We will think in this closing chapter of that cross which has to be taken up day by day, for a Christian, as Luther says, is a Crucian. The Saviour pictures to His hearers a procession, He Himself taking the lead with His Cross. He is the chief Crucian. All His true disciples follow in this procession. Each has his own particular cross, and the direction of the procession, when one looks far enough, is towards the kingdom of heavenly glory.

The Crusaders used to carry a painted cross on their shoulders, and some talk of bearing a cross which sits just as lightly. It is to them a mere thing of ornament; a passport to respectability, for there is a cross which has become fashionable, and from which all trace of suffering and self-denial has disappeared.

That is not the character of the cross of which Christ spoke to His disciples. The life to which He calls us, and the path along which He leads, is characterized by cross-bearing from beginning to end. In outward appearance the cross varies, but it is always something which crosses self, and frees us from our own self-will. It is therefore the way to rest, for the only place in the wide world in which the soul can find true rest is in taking up the yoke or cross of Christ. In doing our own will there is never rest, but in yielding to the will of another there is. "The soul abiding under this cross comes into the true, pure, and perfect liberty, where it hath scope unto holiness, freedom unto righteousness, and is in strait bonds and holy chains from all liberty to the flesh, and from all unholiness and unrighteousness of every kind."[1]

Someone has described this cross-bearing life as a *spread-out surrender,* a surrender which covers our whole sphere of action, and lasts all our days. It is often in little things that Christ asks us to deny ourselves, and it would be far easier for some to take up a great cross and die once upon it than to take up these little crosses day by day and die a *deeper* death upon them. So the word "daily" becomes to some, what Christ's Cross was to the Jews, a stone of stumbling and a rock of offence.

Yet, as we have already suggested, it is only in this cross-bearing life, in ever yielding our will to our Lord, that we find rest and peace. The way of the Cross is the royal way, and they who tread it are kings and priests unto God. It is always to those who tread it the way of glory as it was to Christ, "Who for the joy that was set before Him, endured the Cross, despising the shame." It was because of this that Paul gloried in tribulation, "knowing that tribulation worketh patience; and patience, experience; and experience hope: and hope maketh not ashamed; because the love of God is shed abroad in our hearts by the Holy Ghost, which is given unto us" (Rom. 5:3-5). "He that hath suffered in the flesh hath ceased from sin."

On several occasions art has been sanctified to illustrate this. In one picture, for example, a bit of moorland stretches its lonely waste away into the distance, and slopes up to the white hills beyond. In the foreground, a few scattered shrubs have forced their way among the rocks so sharp for tender feet. Up from the valley, over which dark clouds hover, a young woman comes with slow, sad step and serious mien. From a rift in the sky above her, a softened light falls upon a cross at her feet. A cross, before whose rude weight her delicate shoulders shrink. At her side, all unseen, the Saviour, who has guided her to this lonely spot, stands watching her. Not with bowed form and marred visage, not as the Man of Sorrows, but as her Risen Lord has He come. Clad in a robe of spotless white, which falls from throat to sandaled feet, He bends on her a look in which patient love and steadfast purpose, and tender pity, are most divinely blended. As He stands there watching, waiting, the figure starts to life from the canvas, and we hear in melting tones, "Christ hath many lovers of His kingdom, and but few bearers of His cross!" No longer do the timid steps falter. Lines of resignation gather about the brave mouth. With her beautiful hair blown back from her serious face, her sweet eyes, "homes of silent prayer," her whole figure expressive of the most touching humility, she stoops to raise it.

But lo! the wondrous change! A moment ago there lay before her misty eyes only the cross's rugged form and weary weight. But now, with the clearer vision granted in her hour of submission, she sees clusters of dewy roses clinging to it lovingly. They hide the rude outline. They lay their velvet petals caressingly over the sharp edges. They open their golden hearts, and with prodigal sweetness throw their perfume all abroad upon the air. They lighten the ponderous weight. They shield her from the harsh touch. They brighten and beautify the pathway which promised to be so dark and lonely.

Ah! the artist has done more than simply to symbolize a glowing idea. With his magic brush he has broken into these brilliant hues the white light of an immortal truth. They who have borne Christ's Cross can testify how rich and full it has made their life; how blessed beyond all others are they upon whom it is laid. With that mysterious blending of the will in Christ, peace flows into the soul like an unbroken river. To a heart beating ever in accord, through Him, with nature's symphonies, the common things of life lose their meanness, and there comes daily a new "splendor in the grass, and glory in the flower."

Who could ever read Samuel Rutherford's letters without noting how this aspect of the daily cross was ever before him! Listen: "He that looketh unto the white side of the cross, and taketh it up handsomely, findeth it just such a burden unto him *as wings are to a bird.*" . . . "I find that His sweet presence eateth out the bitterness of sorrow and suffering. I think it is a sweet thing that Christ saith of my cross, 'Half Mine!' and that He divideth these sufferings with me, and taketh the larger share to Himself; nay, that I and my whole cross are wholly Christ's.". . . "Some have one cross, some seven, some ten, some half a cross. Yet all the saints have whole and full joy; and seven crosses have seven joys. I find the very frowns of Christ's wooing sweet and lovely. I had rather have Christ's buffet and love-stroke than another king's kiss. Speak evil of Christ who will, I hope to die with love thoughts of Him.". . . " I have neither tongue nor pen to express the sweetness and excellency of the love of Christ. My chains are gold. Christ's Cross is all over-gilded and perfumed: His prison is the garden and orchard of my delights. I would go through burning quick to my lovely Christ.". . . "I give under my own handwriting to you a testimonial of Christ and His

Cross, that they are a sweet couple, and that Christ hath never yet been set in His own due chair of honor amongst us all." . . . "I find crosses, Christ's carved work that He marketh out for us, and that with crosses He figureth and portrayeth us to His own image, cutting away pieces of our ill and corruption. Lord cut, Lord carve, Lord wound, Lord do anything that may perfect Thy Father's image in us, and make us meet for glory." . . . "Oh, how sweet a sight it is to see a cross betwixt Christ and us, to hear our Redeemer say, at every sigh, and every blow, and every loss of a believer, 'Half Mine!' So they are called 'the sufferings of *Christ,*' and 'the reproach of *Christ.*' As when two are partners and own-ers of a ship, the half of the gain and half of the loss belong to each of the two; so Christ in our sufferings is half-gainer and half-loser with us. Yea, the heaviest end of the black tree of the cross lieth on your Lord: it first falleth on Him, but it reboundeth off Him upon you: and if your cross come through Christ's fingers ere it come to you, it receiveth a fair luster from Him; it getteth a taste and relish of the King's spikenard, and of heaven's perfume. And half of the gain, when Christ's shipful of gold cometh home, shall be yours."

The threefold repetition of the word "cannot" in Luke 14 is sug-gestive. Unless we live this cross-bearing life we cannot be His disciples (verses 26, 27, 33). It is not that we "shall not" but "cannot" be. In other words, this is an unalterable law of discipleship. The only pos-sible way by which we can do the will of God, and live out the ideal Christian life, is by the absolute surrender of ourselves to our Divine Lord. Without this absolute surrender, which, as we have said, is spread out over the whole of our life, we may come after Christ outwardly, we may be called by His name, but we "cannot" be His disciples any more than a bird can fly without wings. On the other hand, as that famous Crucian, Rutherford, says: "If we take up the cross handsomely, we shall find it just such a burden as wings are to a bird."

In bearing patiently the little contradictions, the slight inconve-niences, the trifling losses so frequently encountered, the daily cross will become our daily bread. The nourishment of our life will be to do the will of God as it comes to us in those things that were once trivial *annoyances,* but are now opportunities of saying a continual *Amen* to the will of God. Herein is meat which the world knows not of, and in accepting that will the soul find perfect rest and complete satisfaction.

Let us beware of self-made crosses. We need never go out of our way to find them, and those which we make for ourselves are double crosses, because, being outside the will of God, they bring no strength, consolation, or fruit. Such are all crosses which arise from uneasy fears about the future. We have no right to anticipate His dispensations, or attempt to supply the place of His providence by a providence of our own. "How long shall I have to lie here, doctor?" asked the patient, at the commencement of a weary illness; and the Christian physician could not have given a more suitable answer: "Only one day at a time!"

> Charge not thyself with the weight of a year—
> Child of the Master, faithful and dear—
> Choose not the cross for the coming week;
> For that is more than He bids thee seek.
> Bend not thine arms for tomorrow's load;
> That thou may'st leave to thy gracious God.
> "Day by day" ever He saith to thee,
> "Take up thy cross and follow Me."

Let us then welcome the daily cross, and ask as each morning dawns, How may I deny myself for Christ today; and as the evening shadows gather around us, and we lie down to rest, to be carried on even in our sleep by the gales of the Holy Ghost, let our question be, "Have I found rest and joy and glory today in bearing my daily cross?"

# Notes

**Chapter 2**
1. 2 Corinthians—*Expositors' Bible,* pp. 240-242.
2. *Spirit of Love,* p. 107.

**Chapter 3**
1. *Memoranda Sacra,* p. 24.

**Chapter 4**
1. *Day of Rest,* 1875, p. 326

**Chapter 6**
1. *Epistles St. John,* pp. 38, 102.
2. Pope's *Compendium,* Vol. 2, p. 30.
3. Finney's *Theology,* p. 282.

**Chapter 7**
1. Imitatio Christi," Chapter 13.
2. Dr. Burt Pope, *Sermons and Addresses,* p. 302.

**Chapter 8**
1. Godet, *John,* Vol. 3, p. 70.
2. Professor Findlay, *Galatians,* p. 360.

**Chapter 9**
1. Pere Grou
2. *Week Day Sermons,* p. 210.
3. *Creator and Creature,* p. 397.

**Chapter 10**
1. Beet's *Romans,* p. 181.
2. Beet's *New Life in Christ,* p. 172.
3. Lilias Trotter, *Parables of the Cross.*

**Chapter 12**
1. *Sermons by John Thomas, M.A.,* Vol. 2, p. 126.

**Chapter 14**
1. This sermon is now so difficult of access, owing to the rarity and costliness of the volume which contains it, that we propose to give in this chapter some of its main features, believing they will prove of great value to those who read these pages.

**Chapter 15**
1. *Hibbert Lectures,* p. 65.
2. Findlay, *Galatians,* p. 159.
3. J. Rendel Harris, *Union with God,* p. 142.
4. See Murray's *Holiest of All.*

**Chapter 16**
1. Bowen's *Love Revealed,* p. 186.

**Chapter 17**
1. Professor Upham, *Life of Faith,* p. 192.
2. John Ruskin.
3. *Lectures on Ephesians,* p. 319.

**Chapter 21**
1. Dr. Robert F. Horton.

**Chapter 23**
1. Isaac Pennington.

*Also from Kingsley Press:*

# THE AWAKENING

## By Marie Monsen

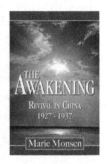

REVIVAL! It was a long time coming. For twenty long years Marie Monsen prayed for revival in China. She had heard reports of how God's Spirit was being poured out in abundance in other countries, particularly in nearby Korea; so she began praying for funds to be able to travel there in order to bring back some of the glowing coals to her own mission field. But that was not God's way. The still, small voice of God seemed to whisper, "What is happening in Korea can happen in China if you will pay the price in prayer." Marie Monsen took up the challenge and gave her solemn promise: "Then I will pray until I receive."

*The Awakening* is Miss Monsen's own vivid account of the revival that came in answer to prayer. Leslie Lyall calls her the "pioneer" of the revival movement—the handmaiden upon whom the Spirit was first poured out. He writes: "Her surgical skill in exposing the sins hidden within the Church and lurking behind the smiling exterior of many a trusted Christian—even many a trusted Christian leader—and her quiet insistence on a clear-cut experience of the new birth set the pattern for others to follow."

The emphasis in these pages is on the place given to prayer both before and during the revival, as well as on the necessity of self-emptying, confession, and repentance in order to make way for the infilling of the Spirit.

One of the best ways to stir ourselves up to pray for revival in our own generation is to read the accounts of past awakenings, such as those found in the pages of this book. Surely God is looking for those in every generation who will solemnly take up the challenge and say, with Marie Monsen, "I will pray until I receive."

Buy online at our website: **www.KingsleyPress.com**
Also available as an eBook for Kindle, Nook and iBooks.

# The Revival We Need

## *by Oswald J. Smith*

When Oswald J. Smith wrote this book almost a hundred years ago he felt the most pressing need of the worldwide church was true revival—the kind birthed in desperate prayer and accompanied by deep conviction for sin, godly sorrow, and deep repentance, resulting in a living, victorious faith. If he were alive today he would surely conclude that the need has only become more acute with the passing years.

The author relates how there came a time in his own ministry when he became painfully aware that his efforts were not producing spiritual results. His intense study of the New Testament and past revivals only deepened this conviction. The Word of God, which had proved to be a hammer, a fire and a sword in the hands of apostles and revivalists of bygone days, was powerless in his hands. But as he prayed and sought God in dead earnest for the outpouring of the Holy Spirit, things began to change. Souls came under conviction, repented of their sins, and were lastingly changed.

The earlier chapters of the book contain Smith's heart-stirring messages on the need for authentic revival: how to prepare the way for the Spirit's moving, the tell-tale signs that the work is genuine, and the obstacles that can block up the channels of blessing. These chapters are laced with powerful quotations from revivalists and soul-winners of former times, such as David Brainerd, William Bramwell, John Wesley, Charles Finney, Evan Roberts and many others. The latter chapters detail Smith's own quest for the enduement of power, his soul-travail, and the spiritual fruit that followed.

In his foreword to this book, Jonathan Goforth writes, "Mr. Smith's book, *The Revival We Need,* for its size is the most powerful plea for revival I have ever read. He has truly been led by the Spirit of God in preparing it. To his emphasis for the need of a Holy Spirit revival I can give the heartiest amen. What I saw of revival in Korea and in China is in fullest accord with the revival called for in this book."

Buy online at our website: **www.KingsleyPress.com**
Also available as an eBook for Kindle, Nook and iBooks.

# A Present Help
## By Marie Monsen

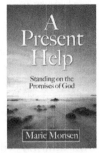

Does your faith in the God of the impossible need reviving? Do you think that stories of walls of fire and hosts of guardian angels protecting God's children are only for Bible times? Then you should read the amazing accounts in this book of how God and His unseen armies protected and guided Marie Monsen, a Norwegian missionary to China, as she traveled through bandit-ridden territory spreading the Gospel of Jesus Christ and standing on the promises of God. You will be amazed as she tells of an invading army of looters who ravaged a whole city, yet were not allowed to come near her mission compound because of angels standing sentry over it. Your heart will thrill as she tells of being held captive on a ship for twenty-three days by pirates whom God did not allow to harm her, but instead were compelled to listen to her message of a loving Savior who died for their sin. As you read the many stories in this small volume your faith will be strengthened by the realization that our God is a living God who can still bring protection and peace in the midst of the storms of distress, confusion and terror—a very present help in trouble.

Buy online at our website: **www.KingsleyPress.com**
Also available as an eBook for Kindle, Nook and iBooks.

Made in the USA
Coppell, TX
21 February 2024

29258093R00089